The

Complete

Collector's

Guide to

Shells
& Shelling

Sandra Romashko

Seashells from
the Waters of the
North American
Atlantic and
Pacific Oceans,
Gulf of Mexico,
Gulf of California,
The Caribbean,
The Bahamas,
and Hawaii

Windward Publishing

AN IMPRINT OF FINNEY COMPANY

4th Edition
Copyright © 2004 Sandra D. Romashko

Previous Editions © 1984, 1994, and 1998

ISBN 0-89317-058-5

Library of Congress No. 81-51067

Windward Publishing
AN IMPRINT OF FINNEY COMPANY

3943 Meadowbrook Road
Minneapolis, MN 55426-4505
Phone: (800) 846-7027
www.finney-hobar.com

Printed in the United States of America

5 7 9 10 8 6

Contents

Introduction

The descriptive text and the color photographs are intended to give prominent and easily identifiable characteristics to aid in the identification of each mollusk. However, in attempting to identify specimens, the shell collector must learn to expect some amount of variation in color, size, patterns, and shape from the statistics given in this book. Size measurements are of average mature shells that are most likely to be found. Shape is often quite variable between adult and juvenile snails, and environmental surroundings can affect the size and shape of the shells. Water temperature, diet, water currents and turbidity, and foreign growths can all affect development. Those shells that live and mature in quiet waters are more likely to be larger and more fragile than those in exposed wave-washed areas. Abnormalities in development are not uncommon and in many cases contribute to the value of the specimen. For example, a right-handed specimen of the normally left-handed lightning whelk is rare; or an albino individual of a normally colorful species may be more highly prized.

More than 6,000 species of mollusks are found in American waters. Those included in these accounts are the ones most likely to be found in the littoral zone or in shallow waters or those that are particularly favored as collectors' specimens because of size, color, or beauty. The gastropods and bivalves are arranged in order of evolutionary development within their class, starting with the most primitive or earliest species. Reevaluation of scientific names of species occurs constantly; those used in this text are the most recent and generally accepted classifications, but references to former or other classifications are included.

Along with the description of each mollusk, the value of the shell is included. The first shell collectors, thousands of years ago, wondered what the shells they found were worth—either in terms of barter, food value, practical use, or adornment. American Indians of the northeast coast made wampum from hard-shell clams, whelks, and periwinkles; Indians living on the Pacific coast of the United States used tusk shells as currency. The values listed are intended to be a guide to the price you can expect to pay or get when buying or selling shells. Prices of individual shells of the same species will vary depending on size, condition, scarcity, and demand. However, some uncommon shells may not be worth much if they are not particularly attractive or interesting; and some usually common shells may demand a surprising price because of their size or because they are heavily collected and in demand. Therefore, consider the listed prices a guideline, knowing full well that you may be asked to pay more, and may pay it, for that shell you simply must have in your collection.

natural history of
Phylum Mollusca

Members of this group are casually classified as "shelled animals." The shell is the product of the mantle, a thin sheet of muscular flesh that envelopes the vital organs of the animal and in some species can cover the back and sides of the shell like a skirt. The mantle has many pores through which the animal secretes a thin limy substance that solidifies quickly into a thin layer. Layers are built up one upon the other, often crosswise, until the mass is built up into the shell. Often the surface is "final coated" by the animal with a thin porcelain-like finish. The outer edges of the mantle continue to secrete, allowing the shell to grow in width and length, while pores in the mantle within the shell add to the thickness of the shell and also perform any necessary repairs.

In some species, the interior walls are made of alternating layers of lime and horny tissue—shinglelike lime crystals. When light is reflected from the edges of these microscopic shingles, the luster produced is known as mother-of-pearl.

In addition to the mantle, the body of the mollusk also consists of the head, the foot, and visceral mass. The head is well developed and distinct in the snails and squids but is not defined in the bivalves. Also, the gastropods have a ribbonlike set of teeth known as the radula in the mouth cavity. These teeth are absent in the bivalves. Within the visceral mass are contained the circulatory, respiratory, reproductive, digestive, and excretive organs. Waste ducts from the paired kidneys and intestine open into the mantle cavity. Mollusks have a two-chambered heart that circulates colorless or blue blood. Most have separate sexes, but there are many hermaphroditic species. Most mollusks reach their mature size in one to six years.

Six Classes of the Phylum Mollusca

1. The class Monoplacophora contains primarily extinct fossil species—there are only five living deep-sea species. They are limpet-like in shape, have paired internal organs and gills, lack eyes and tentacles, and have a single row of radular teeth.

2. The chitons, class Amphineura, have a shell made up of eight plates enclosed by a leathery border, the girdle, which holds the plates in place. They have a large broad foot and a head that lacks eyes and tentacles but has a well-developed radula. They are sluggish, preferring shallow water where they adhere to rocks by means of the flat foot. Sexes are separate; most are herbivorous, but some species are carnivores.

3. Univalves or snails belong to the class Gastropoda, which has the greatest number of members of the entire phylum. These animals have a single shell, which is usually coiled or caplike; some are shell-less. They have a distinct head, most with a radula, two eyes, and well-developed tentacles, and many have an operculum. Representatives of this class can be found in salt or fresh water or on land as air-breathing animals. The aquatic species have gills, and the land snails have a modified "lung." Univalves can be either herbivorous or carnivorous; many are hermaphroditic, and some have sex reversal.

4. The class Pelecypoda includes the bivalves, which have a pair of shells joined by a hinge and held together by strong internal muscles. A head is lacking, but the animal feeds upon minute plant and animal matter that is drawn into the shell through one siphon and expelled through another siphon. There is a muscular foot, which is used for burrowing or for attachment to rocks or coral by the immobile species. All of the members of this second-largest class of mollusks are aquatic, and most are marine species. In most species, the sexes are separate, but some like the scallops are hermaphroditic and still others have sex reversal.

5. Tusk shells are in the class Scaphopoda. These elongated mollusks have long tapered conical shells that are slightly curved and open at both ends. They live buried in mud with the small end of the shell sticking up into the water. The larger posterior end contains a foot; there is no true head, but eyes, gills, and radula exist. The sexes are separate in this exclusively marine group.

6. Another entirely marine class, Cephalopoda, includes the squids, octopuses, nautiluses, and spirulas. These are highly specialized invertebrates that are extremely fast and have good vision. All of them have a head with a parrot-like beak that is surrounded by long prehensile tentacles covered by suckers. The majority of the species are predators; the sexes are separate.

iii

Collecting Shells

While occasionally a beautiful shell specimen will be washed up onto a beach by a gentle wave, coastal areas will more likely be strewn with broken and bleached shells. Most prized specimens are obtained by collecting live mollusks. Since they are primarily nocturnal, mollusks can be effectively sought at night on beaches during low tide with the aid of a bright light. Beachcombing during daylight can produce results, but rocks will have to be overturned, crevices and protected areas inspected, and natural covers of seaweeds and grasses scrutinized. Divers with the aid of a snorkel are likely to find that exploring shallow waters will be productive. In any case, an experienced eye will contribute to success, since live specimens are likely to be camouflaged by algae and marine growths and hidden by other invertebrates and their surroundings.

Caution—some areas and waters are protected by federal or state laws. It is imperative that the shell collector find out about any regulations protecting mollusks and reefs. And even if the area is not protected, the shell collector has an obligation to protect and restore the habitat—do not disturb the environment any more than absolutely necessary, replace any rocks or cover that was moved, and do not over collect!

Dredging is a productive way to collect specimens from sandy bottoms. A small handmade dredge can be dragged from the stern of a rowboat or small motor boat. The dredge should be fairly small so that it can still be hauled when it is weighted to dig into the muddy bottom. And while they may not be obvious during dredging, small specimens may be included in the mud that collects in the dredge. Some of the matter should be saved, dried, and inspected for tiny prizes.

Cleaning Shells

Live Specimens

If the specimen was collected alive, the flesh must be cleaned out before it deteriorates and produces offensive odors. There are several ways to clean out live shells.

1. Put the shell in cool salt or fresh water and gradually bring to a boil. Boil gently for about five minutes, so as not to damage the shell. Most of the snails can then be hooked and removed by unwinding them; the shells of the bivalves will gape, allowing easy removal of the fleshy matter.
2. Some can be cleaned alive. If the animal is slightly extended, pierce the muscle with the tines of a fork and pull the animal out with a sharp twist and jerk.
3. Larger snails can be frozen for a few days and then defrosted. The soft parts should then be removed, and the cavity should be flushed thoroughly with water.
4. Heavy specimens can be hung by the foot until the weight of the shell pulls the animal out.
5. In warmer areas, the shell can be buried in dirt for a few days so that ants and other insects can clean out the flesh. Or bury the shell in soft, dry sand where it will rot out after several days. If allowing the snail to rot, be sure the aperture is down so that the shell will not be stained by the decaying matter.
6. Preserve live specimens in a 50% solution of methyl or isopropyl alcohol. After about a week, the animal can be easily removed. Or small shells preserved in alcohol need only be dried.
7. Small, fragile shells can be soaked in water for 2 to 3 days until the flesh has rotted out. Water should be changed frequently during this period.
8. The specimen can also be preserved in formalin. The use of formalin makes it unnecessary to remove the body since the procedure dries and hardens the flesh. You may, however, choose to remove the matter anyway. Soak the shell in a 5% solution of formalin. The formaldehyde solution that is available from drug stores is a 40% solution; mix 1 part with 8 parts water for the proper solution. The dilute formaldehyde solution must be buffered with 1 teaspoon sodium bicarbonate (baking soda) per quart of solution. Soak for several days, after which the animal should be easy to remove.

V

Empty Shells

After the shell is rid of all the animal matter, it may still require cleaning to remove growths or deposits.

1. In many cases, scrubbing the shell in warm, soapy water will clean it sufficiently. If you choose to keep the periostracum on your specimen, this technique is the only additional cleaning method you should use, since bleach or other stronger solutions will dissolve the periostracum. Also, do not subject the operculum to any other cleaning solutions.
2. Soaking the shell in commercial laundry bleach will remove algae and other stains. The soaking time and concentration of bleach can be increased for heavily stained shells.
3. Shells can also be soaked in a strong lye solution. This solution will also remove stains and growths, but in addition, it will loosen calcareous deposits that can then be carefully chipped away.
4. A muriatic acid solution can be used to clean heavily encrusted shells, but this solution is not recommended unless absolutely necessary. The acid reacts with the encrustations on the shell, but it will also react with the shell itself, leaving a hole in the shell or even dissolving the specimen. The shells should be immersed in the muriatic acid for only short periods of time and thoroughly rinsed after each soaking.

After any cleaning method, be sure that the shell is rinsed thoroughly or soaked in fresh water. Any residual chemical can still react with the shell and possibly mar or even destroy it. And, of course, protect your hands and arms from any caustic or acid solution—use forceps or tongs to immerse and remove shells from the cleaning baths.

In all circumstances, be sure to save the operculum so that it can be replaced inside the aperture after the shell has been cleaned and dried. This procedure can be done by gluing the operculum to a wad of cotton and placing it in the opening of the shell.

Bivalves must be cleaned carefully so as not to break the hinge. Clear glue or shellac lightly applied to the hinge will strengthen it. After cleaning, a bivalve can be soaked in a solution of equal parts of glycerine and water and tied shut until dry, which will allow the shell to stay shut; dead bivalves will normally be in the open position.

Once the shells have been cleaned, they can be beautifully displayed almost anywhere—but they should be kept from sunlight, since their color will soon be bleached out. If you choose, apply a light coating of neatsfoot oil to enhance the finish and color.

Chitons

Preparing chitons as specimens requires special treatment; otherwise they roll up into tight balls. The animals should be kept alive in sea water. Put the chiton on a piece of wood or glass in a dish of sea water. When it is in a flattened position, hold the chiton down with your thumb on its back and at the same time pour out the water and replace it with a 70% solution of alcohol. After a couple of minutes, the chiton will remain flat; let it soak for a few days.

Once the chiton is preserved and dried, the fleshy parts can be removed. Do not damage or remove the girdle, which holds the plates in place.

If you prefer to remove, clean, and reassemble the eight plates, simply boil the chiton in water for about five minutes and follow this procedure by soaking the chiton in household bleach for another 30 minutes. Any tissue can now be removed from the plates with a stiff brush. After drying, the plates can be glued together again. The cleaned plates will have a range of colors from white to blue green with markings of yellow, orange, or pink.

Gastropod Shell

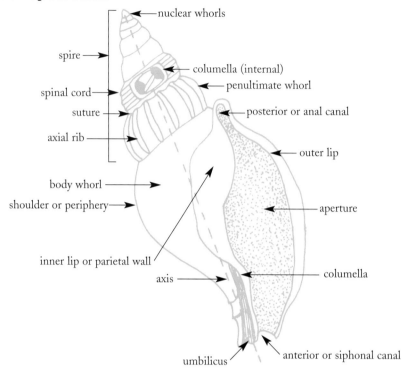

nuclear whorls

spire

spinal cord

suture

axial rib

body whorl

shoulder or periphery

columella (internal)

penultimate whorl

posterior or anal canal

outer lip

aperture

inner lip or parietal wall

axis

columella

umbilicus

anterior or siphonal canal

Bivalve Shell

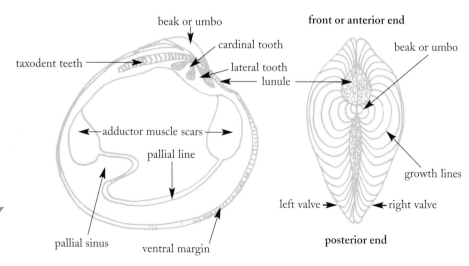

beak or umbo

cardinal tooth

taxodent teeth

lateral tooth

lunule

front or anterior end

beak or umbo

adductor muscle scars

pallial line

growth lines

left valve

right valve

pallial sinus

ventral margin

posterior end

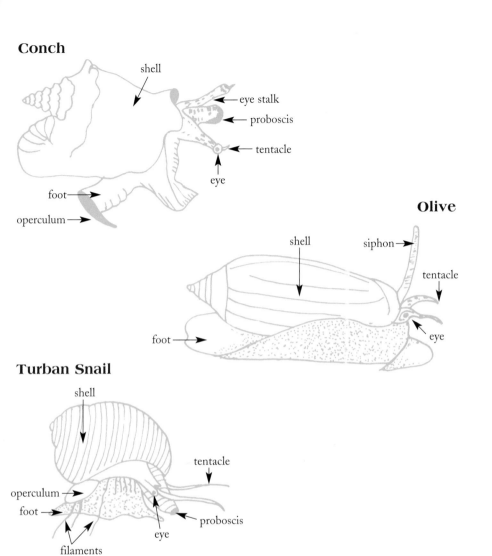

Conch

shell

eye stalk

proboscis

tentacle

eye

foot

operculum

Olive

shell

siphon

tentacle

foot

eye

Turban Snail

shell

tentacle

operculum

foot

eye

proboscis

filaments

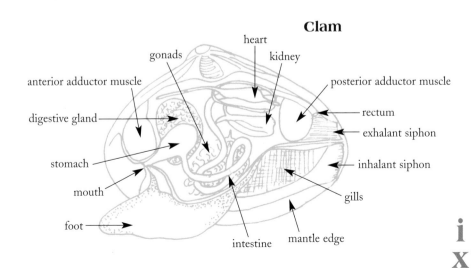

Clam

heart

gonads

kidney

anterior adductor muscle

posterior adductor muscle

digestive gland

rectum

exhalant siphon

stomach

inhalant siphon

mouth

foot

gills

intestine

mantle edge

Location Map

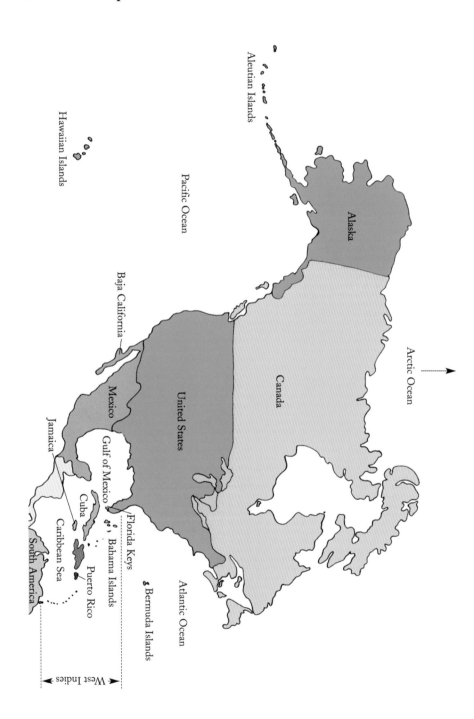

Class:
Gastropoda

Abalones { Family :: Haliotidae }

Abalones have very small spires, the majority of the shell being the body whorl. There are four to six natural holes along the left margin that are used by the animal to expel water and waste. The inside of the shell has an iridescent or pearl-like appearance, often multicolored. The abalones are commonly found in shallow water but can be found in depths to 1,200 ft. (366 m), clinging to rocks and other underwater growth with such surprising tenacity that they must be removed with the aid of a pry bar. All are edible; in fact, they are so heavily fished that state laws control harvesting and restrict the legal size of possession. The size of the abalones ranges up to 12 in. (305 mm), and they can live 15 to 20 years.

Corrugated or Pink Abalone

Haliotis corrugata, Wood. The color of this shell varies from dark green to reddish brown and is characterized by strong ribbing, 2 to 4 high-rimmed holes, and the scalloped edge; the inside is mother-of-pearl. It is found among seaweeds in moderately shallow water from southern California to Baja California. It is a fairly common species and is 6 to 10 in. (152 to 254 mm) in length. . . . . $12–$18

Green Abalone

Haliotis fulgens, Philippi. The thick, greenish brown to brown shell has 5 to 7 open perforations and prominent, closely spaced spiral ribs. The interior is blue green to pink mother-of-pearl. Uncommon due to overharvesting, the shell is found from southern California to Baja California in moderately shallow water and is 6 to 8 in. (152 to 203 mm) long. . . . . $15–$28

Red Abalone

Haliotis rufescens, Swainson. This reddish brown species is one of the largest of our abalones, reaching 10 in. (254 mm) or more in size. The heavy shell is sometimes encrusted and has 3 to 4 open holes along the margin and a red edge along the outer rim; the interior is pale. It is found on rocks in moderately shallow water along the U.S. Pacific coast from Washington to Baja California. The red abalone is fairly common and is the most commercially important of the abalones. . . . . $5–$25
More than 9 in. (229 mm) . . . . $100–$150

Keyhole limpets are conical-shaped shells with an oval-shaped base and a hole at the apex in the adult. Young specimens have a slit in the anterior edge of the shell, but the slit fills as growth proceeds until the slit is a hole in the top of the adult shell. The slit, or keyhole, is used to expel water and waste, corresponding to the holes in the shell of the abalone. Keyhole limpets feed at night on algae-covered rocks in the intertidal zone. Most species are vegetarians, but some are carnivores.

Rough Keyhole Limpet
Diodora aspera, Rathke. The gray to yellowish shell often has dark radial rays; the interior is plain white with a callus around the hole. A common species, this shell is found on rocks from the low-tide line to moderately shallow water along the west coast of the U.S. from southern Alaska to Baja California. Its length is 1 to 2 in. (25 to 50 mm) long. . . . . $2–$5

Lister's Keyhole Limpet
Diodora listeri, d'Orbigny. Found on rocks at the low-tide line, Lister's limpet is dirty white to gray with prominent radial ribs forming a rough exterior. Common from Florida to the West Indies, the shell may reach 2 in. (50 mm) in length. . . . . $1–$2

Barbados Keyhole Limpet
Fissurella barbadensis, Gmelin. Distinguished from other limpets by the green interior, the shell has many prominent irregular ribs, varying in color from gray to purplish. A very common species from south Florida to the West Indies and to Brazil, the 1³⁄₄ to 1¹⁄₂ in. (20 to 40 mm) long shell is found in the intertidal zone but is often covered with algae and may go unnoticed.   less than $1–$2

White Keyhole Limpet
Fissurella gemmata, Menke. Previously classified as *Fissurella alba*, Carp. A narrow black rim encircles the thick callus around the hole, while the external color is white or light gray. It is a common shell, little more than 1 in. (30 mm) long, and is found in shallow water in the southern Gulf of California. . . . . $2–$4

Knobby Keyhole Limpet

Fissurella nodosa, Born. The exterior of the shell is grayish to brownish with strong radial ribs and a prominently notched margin. This common species is ³⁄₄ to 1¹⁄₂ in. (20 to 40 mm) long and is found throughout Florida to the West Indies on rocks just below the low-tide line. ...... less than $1–$2

Great Keyhole Limpet

Megathura crenulata, Sowerby. This largest known keyhole limpet reaches a length of 4 in. (102 mm) and has a keyhole approximately one-sixth of its length. The animal has a dark gray to black mantle, which is large enough to cover the entire shell. The shell is brownish, and the keyhole is encircled in white. This limpet is a common edible species, but it is becoming scarcer due to over harvesting. It is found in shallow water on rocks from the low-tide line out, and on breakwaters from central California to Baja California. .... $6–$8
100 mm+ .... $18–$30

True Limpets { Family :: Acmaediae }

True limpets have a conical shell without any hole or slit. The height and shape of the shell is influenced by the environment: those in exposed areas and subject to heavy wave action have low shells; those that adhere to seaweed have more elongated shells. Most species inhabit the intertidal area where they feed at night among rocks on microscopic plant life. They may reach 4 in. (102 mm) across, and they move by means of a single broad muscular foot. Limpets are eaten in some places.

File Limpet

Acmaea lima-tula, Carpenter. Also listed as *Collisella lima-tula*. The midheight oval shell is dark greenish black and about 1 in. (25 mm) across. It is commonly found on rocks in the intertidal zone on the Pacific coast from the Puget Sound to Mexico. .... less than $1–$2

Black Limpet

Cellana exarata, Nuttall. The oval, moderately arched shell is marked with distinct black radiating ribs with lighter color between the ribs. It reaches a length of 1¹⁄₂ in. (38 mm) and is found among rocks near shore in Hawaii, where it is also sold in fish markets as *opihi*. This shell is common. .... $2–$3

Giant Owl Limpet

Lottia gigantea, Sowerby. This largest North American true limpet, reaching 3 to 4 in. (76 to 102 mm) in length, is named for the bluish "owl-shaped" markings on the interior of the shell. The slightly arched oval shell is mottled brown or gray black with a rough surface. It is common on rocks between tide lines on coasts from California to Mexico. The foot is edible. . . . . $4–$7

Top Shells { Family :: Trochidae }

These shells are largely composed of iridescent mother-of-pearl, which may be concealed on the outer shell by various pigmentations, but the insides retain the pearly luster. They have a thin horny operculum, that is made up of many whorls. Top shells are vegetarians, feeding by means of many radulae. They range in size from $\frac{1}{8}$ to 6 in. (3 to 150 mm) across and are found among rocks and seaweed in shallow water or, some species, in great depths.

Top Shell

Calliostoma bonita, Strong, Hanna, and Hertlein. This small tan shell is found on the Pacific coast, primarily in Baja California. It reaches less than 1 in. (24 mm) across. This species lives on kelp beds offshore; it is fairly common. . . . . $1–$2

Channeled Top Shell

Calliostoma canaliculatum, Lightfoot. The thin strong shell ranges in color from a yellowish tan to a rich brown. This fairly common shell is found in seaweed offshore on the Pacific coast from Alaska to southern California. It attains $1\frac{1}{2}$ in. (38 mm) in length. . . . . $6–$18

Sculptured Top Shell

Calliostoma euglyptum, A. Adams. This dingy white shell is mottled with red and brown and is found along the Atlantic coast from North Carolina to Florida and around to Texas. It is found in sand in shallow to moderately deep water. This common species has a strong shell about 1 in. (25 mm) high. . . . . $7–$8

Calliostoma iris, Pilsbry. This small cream-colored shell is found off Florida's east coast. Fairly common, it reaches $\frac{1}{2}$ in. (13 mm) across. $3

Chocolate-Lined Top Shell

Calliostoma javanicum, Lamarck. Previously classified as *C. zonamestum*, A. Adams. This tan-colored shell has 5 to 7 fine, chocolate brown lines. It is about 1 in. (25 mm) across. This rather rare species is found from southern Florida to the West Indies in coral sand in shallow water. . . . . $6–$18

Jujube Top Shell

Calliostoma jujubinum, Gmelin. Shell color varies from brown to red, with white specks above the suture. It reaches 1 in. (25 mm) in height. The shell is fairly common in its range along the Atlantic coast from North Carolina to Florida and to the West Indies. It inhabits seaweeds and sand in shallow water and is commonly washed up on sandy shores. . . . . $2–$8

Western Ribbed Top Shell

Calliostoma ligatum, Gould. This solid brown shell has rounded whorls and 6 to 8 large tan threads. Its range extends from Alaska to California, and it is found in shallow water among stones and algae. A common shell, it is usually under 1 in. (25 mm) high. . . . . $2–$8

Granulose Top Shell

Calliostoma supragranosum, Carpenter. Some specimens of this glossy pale brown shell are beaded near the sutures; others have white spots. Usually less than ½ in. (13 mm) high, they are found among rocks in the intertidal zone from Monterey, California, to Baja California. They are fairly common. . . . . $2–$4

West Indian Top Shell

Cittarium pica, Linné. Previously classified as *Livona pica*. This heavy rough shell is marked with purplish black and white zigzag markings. The horny operculum is round and greenish blue in live animals. A large shell, it can attain 4 in. (102 mm) in height. It is found in shallow water among rocks in the intertidal zone in the West Indies. Specimens may be found in southern Florida, but it is extinct there; it is also found in old Indian shell mounds. The species is common in the West Indies.

. . . . less than $1–$4
More than 3 in. (76 mm) $15

Superb Gaza

Gaza superba, Dall. This shell is a shiny yellowish gray, with the last whorls a lighter straw color with a pinkish sheen. The light but strong shell has rounded whorls and reaches 1 to 1½ in. (25 to 38 mm) across. Found in deep water from the Gulf of Mexico to the West Indies, it is not easy to obtain but is found by dredging. . . $40–$75

Vortex Margarite

Margarites vorticiferus, Dall. This low shell has rapidly expanding whorls and many circular threads. It is pinkish to brown and ⅜ to ⅞ in. (10 to 22 mm) across. The shell is common, found offshore in deep water from Alaska to southern California. . . . . $1–$15

Channeled Solarielle

Solariella lacunella, Dall. This very small shell is ⅛ to ⅜ in. (3 to 10 mm) in size. It is thick and is white to pearl gray. The whorls have six spiral cords, and the top three are beaded. The shell is common, found in sand or rubble in shallow to moderately deep water from Virginia to Key West, Florida. . . . . $4–$5

Smooth Atlantic Tegula

Tegula fasciata, Born. The color is extremely variable, from yellowish to grayish pink and mottled with red, brown, and black. About ½ in. (13 mm) high, the shell is smooth and sometimes shiny, and there may be two teeth at the base of the columella. It is common and is found in shallow water under rocks in its range from south Florida to the West Indies. . . . . less than $1–$2

Rough Top Shell

Tegula rugosa, A. Adams. About ¾ in. (19 mm) across, this solid shell is mottled gray, sometimes with pink markings and occasionally dark bars on a pinkish background. It is a common shell, found in the Gulf of California in moderately shallow water. . . . . $1–$2

Members of this family are solid, heavy shells and have a strong calcareous operculum. The shells are top shaped; the surface is generally brightly colored, but the texture varies and can be smooth or spiny. They feed in shallow water on marine algae and are primarily a tropical family.

Star Arene

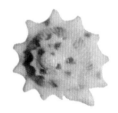

Arene cruentata, Mühlfeld. A small shell, easily identified by the 4 to 5 sharply angled whorls with prominent triangular spines, it is about ½ in. (13 mm) across and ¼ in. (6 mm) high. The outside is white, flecked with red or brown, and the operculum is covered with tiny beads. This uncommon shell is found under rocks in shallow water from southeast Florida to the West Indies. $1–$10

American Star Shell

Astraea americana, Gmelin. Also listed as *Astraea tecta americana.* About 1 in. (25 mm) high, the shell has a pointy apex. It is whitish and is heavy. The 7 to 8 whorls have axial riblets. The white operculum usually has an indentation. This shell is common, found in grass and under rocks in shallow water at low tide in southeast Florida.   . $1–$2

Carved Star Shell

Astraea caelata, Gmelin. The shell is conical in shape and is strong. It reaches 3 in. (76 mm) in height. The rough outer surface is greenish white mottled with red and has both prominent oblique ribs and revolving ribs. The heavy operculum is whitish and calcareous. It is a common shell, found in shallow water among coral rubble and reefs in southeast Florida and the West Indies. . . . . $2–$5

juvenile

Long-Spined Star Shell

Astraea phoebia, Röding. Previously classified as *Astraea longispina,* Lamarck. Yellowish to pale tan in color, this shell is 1 to 2½ in. (25 to 64 mm) across, and it is low, only about half as high. It is characterized by the triangular spines that project from the shell. The shell is a common species, found in grassy shallows from southeast Florida to the West Indies. . . . . $2–$20

Star Shell

Astraea phoebia spinulosa, Röding. Previously classified as *Astraea longispina spinulosa*, Lamarck. This shell is a sub-species of the long-spined star shell, the primary variation being the length of the spines, which are shorter on *A. p. spinulosa*. The shell is common, found in grassy shallow water from southeast Florida to the West Indies.
. . . . less than $1–$2

Green Star Shell

Astraea tuber, Linné. The solid rough shell is about 1½ in. (38 mm) high. It is greenish brown with irregular white blotches and has wide, obliquely vertical ribs. It is common in shallow water on coral reefs from southeast Florida to the West Indies. There is a limy operculum.
. . . . $1–$3

Channeled Turban

Turbo canaliculatus, Hermann. This shell is composed of about 5 well-rounded whorls sculptured with spiral cords. It is named for the strong channeled suture. The smooth finish is checked with green and brown over a lighter greenish-yellow-tan background. It has a heavy operculum and reaches 2 to 3 in. (50 to 76 mm) in height. It is not common, found in moderately shallow water in the Florida Keys and the West Indies.   . . . .$5–$15

Chestnut Turban

Turbo castaneus, Gmelin. The tan beaded surface of this shell is marked with darker brown blotches; occasionally, specimens may have spines and/or be dull green. The shell is solid, has 5 or 6 whorls, and is about 1½ in. (38 mm) high. It is common, found in shallow waters from North Carolina to Florida and Texas and to the West Indies. . . . . $2–$4

Nerites are common tropical shells that are usually found in shallow water among rocks, but they can also be found in brackish water, fresh water, or even on dry land. The shells are small, usually colorful, and generally round in shape.

Bleeding Tooth

Nerita peloronta, Linné. The common name is well suited, based on the appearance of the aperture, which has white teeth surrounded by an orange stain. It can be found among rocks where the animal feeds at night on algae. The 1 to 1½ in. (25 to 38 mm) high shell is common from southern Florida to the West Indies. . . . less than $1–$6

Tessellate Nerite

Nerita tessellata, Gmelin. Another easy to identify nerite, the color is checked dirty white and black; in rare cases, it may be all black. The small shell, ½ to ¾ in. (12 to 19 mm), has a dark operculum. It is common in the intertidal zone from Florida to Texas and to the West Indies. . . . . less than $1–$2

Four-Toothed Nerite

Nerita versicolor, Gmelin. The whitish shell is marked with black and red splotches, and the inner lip usually has four white teeth. About 1 in. (25 mm) high, the thick porcelain-like shell has a grayish pimply operculum. It is common on rocks in intertidal waters from Florida to the West Indies. $3

Netted Nerite

Neritina piratica, Russell. This small shell is less than ¾ in. (20 mm) high. It has a smooth yellowish or olive green surface covered with a network of closely placed black lines resulting in a dotted design. The shell is common, found in brackish water in the West Indies. under $1–$2

Virgin Nerite

Neritina virginea, Linné. Usually less than ½ in. (13 mm) high, this shiny tiny shell occurs in a variety of colors and markings. The inner lip has small irregular teeth; the operculum is smooth. It is very common in brackish water from Florida to Texas and to the West Indies. less than $1–$3

9

Zebra Nerite
Puperita pupa, Linné. This white shell has many black stripes across its surface. It is small, ½ in. (13 mm) high, and has a pale yellow operculum. The aperture is yellow to orange. It is commonly found in rock pools just above the high-tide line throughout southern Florida and the West Indies. .... less than $1–$2

Periwinkles { Family :: Littorinidae }

This large family has worldwide distribution and is littoral, occupying varied habitats including rocks, grasses, pilings, and roots. Different species can tolerate long periods without water and a wide range of water salinity. The sexes are separate; the penis of the male is prominent, and the shape is distinctive enough to aid in identification of the various species. Periwinkles have a chitinous, large operculum that completely covers the aperture when the snail is withdrawn. They feed on microscopic plant life that they scrape up by means of hundreds of rasplike teeth arranged in rows on the long ribbonlike radula. Periwinkles excrete a trail of mucus along their paths, and the head bears a well-developed pair of tentacles, each with an eye at the base.

False Prickly-Winkle
Echininus nodulosus, Pfeiffer. The heavy shell has its whorls marked with revolving rows of pointed knobs and is mottled gray in color. The 1 in. (25 mm) shell is common and found above the high-tide line from Florida to the West Indies. .... $1–$3

Southern Periwinkle
Littorina angulifera, Lamarck. The color of this thin but strong shell is variable. It may be gray, reddish, purplish, or, rarely, yellow or orange. The shell has a horny operculum and is about 1¼ in. (31 mm) high. This species is common and can be found on mangrove roots, leaves, and pilings in shallow water from southern Florida to the West Indies. .... less than $1–$2

Common European Periwinkle

Littorina littorea, Linné. This smooth thick shell is usually brownish to nearly black and is spirally banded with numerous dark bands. The shell is $\frac{1}{2}$ to $1\frac{1}{2}$ in. (13 to 38 mm) high with 6 or 7 whorls. It is extremely common from Labrador to Maryland and in Europe, where it is a favorite food and is often sold roasted in the shell by street vendors. It is believed to be a recently introduced species to the eastern Atlantic Ocean, but specimens more than 1,000 years old have been found in Indian mounds in Nova Scotia. It is found on rocks and in seaweed in the intertidal zone. The female lays eggs in a horny egg capsule that disintegrates, and the young hatch in about a week. . . . . less than $1–$2

Cloudy Periwinkle

Littorina nebulosa, Lamarck. The grayish to yellow shell is occasionally marked with brown spots, and smaller shells often have cloudlike brown and white splotches—the basis for the common name. The $\frac{5}{8}$ to $1\frac{1}{8}$ in. (16 to 28 mm) high shell is found on rocks at the low-tide line in its range from Florida to Texas and the West Indies. . . . . $1–$2

Northern Yellow Periwinkle

Littorina obtusata, Linné. This small smooth shell has virtually no spire. It has 4 whorls; the last is so large that the other whorls scarcely rise above. About $\frac{1}{2}$ in. (13 mm) high, the color is variable, primarily yellow, but it can be orange or brownish yellow and sometimes banded. It is a common shell, found on seaweed in the intertidal zone from Labrador to New Jersey. . . . . less than $1–$2

Northern Rough Periwinkle

Littorina saxatilis, Olivi. The color is variable; the shell can be yellowish or gray to dark brown, and some young specimens can be spotted with yellow or black. About $\frac{1}{2}$ in. (13 mm) high, it has numerous spiral ridges. It is common and is found on rocks in the intertidal zone, often above the water line. It is found on both U.S. coasts from Alaska to Puget Sound and from the Arctic Sea to New Jersey. . . . . less than $1–$2

Zigzag Periwinkle

Littorina ziczac, Gmelin. The shell is whitish with many dark brown or black wavy fine lines; a rare specimen can be blue gray. It is common, found among rocks in the intertidal zone from southeast Florida to the West Indies. . . . . less than $1–$2

Common Prickly Periwinkle or Prickly Winkle
Nodilittorina tuberculata, Menke. This shell is brown and has whorls with several rows of small pointed knobs. It is a common shell and is about ¾ in. (19 mm) high. It is found on rocks in the intertidal zone from southern Florida to the West Indies. .... $1–$3

Beaded Periwinkle
Tectarius muricatus, Linné. The shell is grayish with many spiral rows of small regular white beads. This top-shaped shell is about ¾ in. (19 mm) high. It lives on rocks from the high-tide mark to well out of water. The species can live for long times without water. It is common from the Florida Keys to the West Indies. .... $1–$3

Turrets { Family :: Turritellidae }

A large family with many prized and colorful members, turrets are primarily Pacific shells, but a few species are found in Atlantic waters. The shells are long and slender and may be tightly or loosely coiled.

Boring Turret Shell
Turritella acropora, Dall. Also listed as *Torcula acropora*. The shell can be whitish, pale yellow, or pinky brown with brown mottlings and is 1 to 1½ in. (25 to 38 mm) long. It is a fairly common species, usually found by dredging moderately shallow water. Its range is from North Carolina to Florida and to the West Indies. $1–$2

Cooper's Turret Shell
Turritella cooperi, Carpenter. Also listed as *Haustator cooperi*. This slender shell is about 1½ in. (38 mm) long and is yellowish or light orange, usually with brown streaks. The aperture is normally round. It is fairly common, found in sand in moderately shallow water below the tide line from Monterey to San Diego, California. .... $1–$15

Eastern Turret Shell
Turritella exoleta, Linné. This long slender shell is creamy white splashed with brown splotches and can attain a length of 3 in. (76 mm). It is a common species, found in moderately shallow to deep water from southern Florida to the West Indies. .... $1–$9

Turret Shell

Turritella gonostoma, Valenciennes. The largest western American species, this turret has a strong heavy shell and reaches a length of 6 in. (152 mm). It is bluish gray and heavily marked with brown splotches; there are about 20 flat whorls with fine spiral cords. The shell is fairly common, found in moderately shallow water from the Gulf of California to Peru. .... $1–$6

Knorr's Worm Shell

Vermicularia knorri, Deshayes. The tight, early whorls—the "turritella stage"—of this species are white, while the rest of the loose whorls are yellow brown. This shell reaches a length of 3 in. (76 mm) and is common, found primarily among sponges in shallow water. The range of this shell is from North Carolina to the West Indies. .... $2–$6

Common Worm Shell

Vermicularia spirata, Philippi. The turritella portion is white or brown with the rest of the irregular shell being yellow to reddish brown. It reaches a length of 6 in. (152 mm) and is often found growing with sponges or in colonies intertwined with other individuals. In spite of its appearance, it is a true gastropod, having tentacles, eyes, and radula on the head at the end of the elongated body. The common worm shell is found in shallow waters from Massachusetts to Florida and to the West Indies. .... less than $1

Sundials { Family :: Architectonicidae }

This family is characterized by the broad umbilicus around which coiled whorls give the circular but not elevated shape. Sundials start life as sinistral, or left-handed, larvae, but the nuclear whorls end up hidden at the bottom of the umbilicus as the shell grows and the new whorls coil in the same direction and grow over the apex, resulting in a right-handed shell.

Common Sundial

Architectonica nobilis, Röding. The circular shell is somewhat flattened. It is 1 to 2 in. (25 to 51 mm) in diameter and about ¾ in. (19 mm) high. It is white or gray with brown and purple spots. The whorls have several strong spiral cords and are beaded in the early whorls. It is fairly common and found in shallow water in sand on both coasts: from North Carolina to Florida and Texas and to the West Indies and Brazil, as well as from Baja California to Peru. It is often found washed ashore. $1–$4

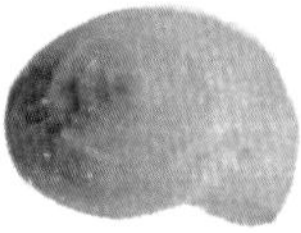

Keeled Sundial
Architectonica peracuta, Dall. This rather small sundial, 3/4 in. (19 mm), is whitish or light gray. It is uncommon and is found from southern Florida to the Gulf of Mexico and to the West Indies. .... $10–more than $50

Slit Worm Shells { Family :: Siliquariidae }

These shells have an open slit along the length of irregular loose coils that allows water to enter the mantle cavity.

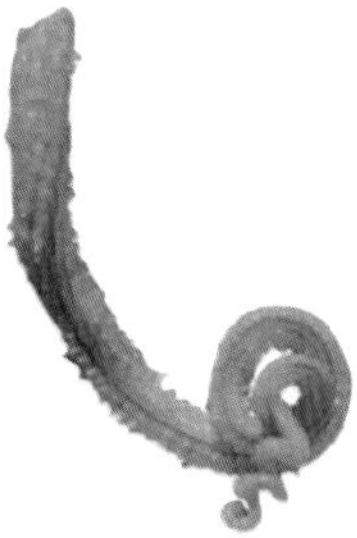

Slit Worm Shell
Siliquaria squamata, Blainville. Previously classified as *Tenagodus squamatus*, Blainville. This 5 to 6 in. (127 to 152 mm) species is grayish to light yellow with the early whorls being smooth and having spines on the later whorls. They are found in sponges in moderately shallow water from North Carolina to Florida and the West Indies. .... $5–$12

Modulus { Family :: Modulidae }

The porcelain-like shells resemble miniature top shells. The base of the columella ends in a sharp toothlike spine.

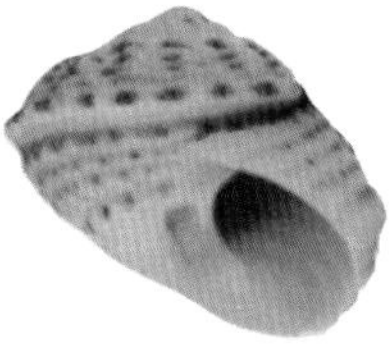

Atlantic Modulus
Modulus modulus, Linné. The yellow-white shell is marked with brown and has low revolving ridges with deep grooves separating the vertical ribs. It is 1/2 to 3/4 in. (12 to 17 mm) in diameter. This shell is very common in shallow water on eelgrass from North Carolina to Florida and Texas and to the West Indies. It is quite variable in appearance. .... less than $1–$2

Horn Shells { Family :: Potamididae }

These are mud dwellers and have elongated, many whorled shells and a horny round operculum.

California Horn Shell
Cerithidea californica, Haldeman. This heavy shell, about 1½ in. (38 mm) long, is dark brown, usually with thin white or yellowish bands and strong axial ribs on the whorls. It is common, found on mud flats from Bolinas Bay, California, to Baja California. .... $1–$2

Horn Shell

Cerithidea montagnei, d'Orbigny. This shiny chocolate brown shell usually has paler bands on the whorls. It is about 1½ in. (38 mm) long. The large aperture has a flaring outer lip, and the whorls have sharp ribs. Found in mud in shallow water, it is common from the Gulf of California to Ecuador. . . . . $1–$2

Wentletraps { Family :: Epitoniidae }

The family has over 200 species, yet almost all are whitish and extremely similar in appearance. They are carnivores, feeding on anemones, corals, and coelenterates.

Lamellose Wentletrap

Epitonium lamellosum, Lamarck. This long slender shell is ⅝ to 1¼ in. (16 to 32 mm) long. It is whitish with some irregular brownish markings. The 7 to 8 whorls have numerous bladelike ribs. The shell is common in southern Florida, the West Indies, and Hawaii. . . . . . $1–$5

Brown-Banded Wentletrap

Epitonium rupicola, Kurtz. The small shell, usually less than 1 in. (25 mm) high, is white or yellowish, usually with 2 brown bands. It is common in sand from the low-tide line to moderately deep water from Cape Cod, Massachusetts, to Florida and Texas. . . . . $1–$6

Janthina Snails { Family :: Janthinidae }

The members of this family are usually violet. They are pelagic and float on the surface buoyed by a mass of bubbles.

Common Purple Sea Snail

Janthina janthina, Linné. This fragile shell is 1 to 1½ in. (25 to 38 mm) in size. It is light purple above the periphery and darker below it. Fairly common, this shell is found worldwide; in the U.S., it can be found south from Nantucket, Massachusetts, and San Diego, California, and in Hawaii. . . . . $1–$6

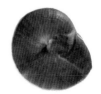

Slipper Shells & Cup-and-Saucer Limpets
{ Family :: Calyptraeidae }

These shells are cap shaped with a shelly shelf or cup on the underside, which supports some of the fleshy parts of the animal. They lack an operculum.

Common Atlantic Slipper Shell
Crepidula fornicata, Linné. The convex shell can be strongly arched or limpetlike. It is light colored and flecked with light brown spots and is about 1½ in. (38 mm) across. On the underside, the shelf covers almost one-half of the shell. This shell is common, found among rocks and on other shells in moderately shallow water from Nova Scotia to Florida and Texas and introduced off the state of Washington. $1

West Indian Cup-and-Saucer
Crucibulum auricula, Gmelin. This cap-shaped shell is whitish or grayish in color. It is 1 in. (25 mm) in diameter, and the cup is virtually freestanding. This shell is uncommon, usually found attached to other shells from North Carolina to Florida and in the West Indies. . . . . less than $1–$2

Carrier Shells { Family :: Xenophoridae }

These flattened top-shaped shells cement pieces of shells, coral, and stones to their own shells so that they look like small piles of debris.

Atlantic Carrier Shell
Xenophora conchyliophora, Born. The unencumbered shell is 1 to 3 in. (25 to 76 mm) across. It is yellowish in color but generally covered by attached objects projecting from the lower edge of the whorls. This shell is uncommon, found on sand near rubble and coral reefs in moderately shallow water from southern Florida to the West Indies and Brazil. . . . . $3–$24

Caribbean Carrier Shell
Xenophora caribaeum, Petit. This thin-shelled large species reaches 3½ in. (89 mm) in size, is whitish in color, and only attaches a few small bits to its shell at the suture line. It is uncommon, found in deep water from the Florida Keys to the West Indies. . . . . $15–$25

True conchs are active snails that have a heavy solid shell with a greatly enlarged body whorl and a clawlike operculum that does not close up the aperture. The expanded outer lip is characteristically notched at the lower end—the "stromboid notch." The last two whorls of the pointed spire have rows of spines. The conchs feed on algae and are found among sea grasses in sand or rocks.

Florida Fighting Conch

Strombus alatus, Gmelin. The solid shell has about 7 whorls and a pointy spire and is 3 to 4 in. (76 to 102 mm) long. It is yellow brown and marked with orange and purple mottlings or bands. The interior is dark brown. Juveniles and immature specimens lack the flaring lip and strongly resemble cone shells. The spire has short spines, and the outer lip slopes downward, differentiating it from the West Indian fighting conch. This shell is a common species, found in shallow water in grassy, sandy areas from North Carolina to Florida, the Gulf of Mexico, and Texas and to the Yucatan. . . . . $4–$6
Purple mouth . . . . $15–$50

Milk Conch

Strombus costatus, Gmelin. The thick heavy white or yellowish shell is covered by a thin periostracum, which is easily removed when the shell is dried. The milk conch is 4 to 6 in. (101 to 152 mm) long and has heavy knobs on the body whorl. The inside of the shell and lip are whitish. This fairly common shell is found in shallow water in grassy, sandy bays and lagoons. Its range is from southeast Florida to the West Indies and to Mexico. . . . . $5–$20
Pink . . . . $12–$25
Lavender $30
Albino $50

Rooster-Tail Conch

Strombus gallus, Linné. The heavy shell is mottled brown, white, and orange. It has a sharp spire and blunt nodes at the shoulders on the body whorl. This uncommon shell reaches a height of 4 to 7 in. (102 to 178 mm) and is found in moderately shallow water from southern Florida to the West Indies. . . . . $7–$35

juvenile

Queen Conch or Pink Conch

Strombus gigas, Linné. This large heavy shell is yellowish white and irregularly marked with brown. It is 7 to 12 in. (178 to 305 mm) high. Fresh specimens have a thin periostracum, which is easily removed when the shell is dried. Most of the shell is the body whorl, and in adults, the outer lip is thick and greatly flaring. The spire is short and conical, and there are blunt nodes on the shoulders. The interior of the shell is bright pink. Juveniles lack the flaring lip and are marked with zigzag brown stripes. The pink conch is one of our largest gastropods and is heavily fished commercially. Found on sandy, grassy bottoms in shallow water, it is normally a common shell, but it is becoming scarcer due to overfishing for food and souvenirs. It is illegal to take or transport any queen conch, alive or dead, from Florida waters or beaches. Its range is from southern Florida to the West Indies. .... $4–$45
Albino $85

West Indian Fighting Conch

Strombus pugilis, Linné. The deep yellow-brown shell reaches a height of 3 to 5 inches (76 to 126 mm) and has an orange aperture. The later whorls have prominent spines, and the outer lip slopes upward, which differentiates it from the Florida fighting conch. Its range is from southeast Florida to the West Indies, where it is common in shallow water. .... $3–$12
More than 4 in. (102 mm) $35

Hawk-Wing Conch

Strombus raninus, Gmelin. The yellow-white shell is marked with brown streaks and blotches. It has a well developed spire and a thick and greatly flaring lip with a deep notch near the bottom. It is 4 to 5 in. (102 to 127 mm) high, and the shoulders of the body whorl have nodes. This shell is a common species, found in shallow water from southern Florida to the West Indies. $2–$15

These highly polished, colorful shells are oval shaped and have a thick-lipped aperture marked with teeth on both sides. They do not have an operculum. Immature specimens are fragile. They lack the curled lip and are usually banded, whereas the adult is spotted.

Atlantic Deer Cowry

Cypraea cervus, Linné. Our largest cowry, it can reach 7 in. (178 mm) in length. It is similar in appearance to the measled cowry, except the deer cowry is more inflated, has a thinner shell, and the small whitish spots lack brown centers. The heavily spotted brown shell has brown apertural teeth. This species is fairly common in shallow water from Florida to the West Indies. $3–$25 More than 5 in. (127 mm). . . . . $6–$250

Atlantic Gray Cowry

Cypraea cinerea, Gmelin. The top of this round, plump cowry is grayish brown diffusing to lilac, and the sides are spotted with blackish brown dots or streaks. The bottom is white and the apertural teeth are small. The shell is 1½ in. (38 mm) long. It is fairly common in shallow water from Florida to the West Indies. . . . . $1–$9

Mouse Cowry

Cypraea mus, Linné. This rather uncommon species is 2 in. (51 mm) in size. It is tan overall with darker wavy lines and is speckled. The outer lip has brown teeth. The shell is found in the southern Caribbean. . . . . $6–$25 More than 1¾ in. (44 mm) . . . . $30–$50

Chestnut Cowry

Cypraea spadicea, Swainson. The back of the whitish shell has a large light chestnut brown spot outlined by an irregular dark brown margin. It is 1 to 2½ in. (25 to 64 mm) in size. The narrow aperture is white, and both lips have teeth. This fairly common shell is found from below the low-tide line to moderately deep water from Monterey, California, to Baja California. . . . . $2–$25

Atlantic Yellow Cowry

Cypraea spurca acicularis, Gmelin. This cowry has strong white teeth on both sides of the aperture. The base is white, and the back is yellowish orange with many white and brown spots. It is ¾ to 1¼ in. (20 to 32 mm) long. This shell is uncommon, found on shallow water reefs from South Carolina to Florida and to the West Indies. $3–$6

Measled Cowry
Cypraea zebra, Linné. The highly polished dark brown cowry has white spots, with the spots on the sides having brown centers. The shell is 2 to 4 ½ in. (51 to 114 mm) long and has brown apertural teeth on both lips. Young specimens have broad bands, which occasionally remain in the adult. The shell is fairly common and is found in shallow water from southeast Florida to the West Indies. . . . . $6–$60

Trivias { Family :: Eratoidae }

Similar in appearance to true cowries, trivias are smaller and characterized by the small ribs that run around the shell from the narrow aperture to the center of the back.

Apple Seed Erato
Erato vitellina, Hinds. This shell is small, about ½ in. (13 mm) long. It is wider at one end, giving it a pear-like appearance. The shell is brown, blotched with purple. The thickened outer lip bears small teeth. This species is common in shallow water from California to Mexico. . . . . $2–$4

Coffee Bean Trivia
Trivia pediculus, Linné. The ⅜ to ¾ in. (10 to 19 mm) long trivia is tan to violet brown with three pairs of irregular brown blotches on the back. It is common, found on coral reefs in shallow water from Florida to the West Indies. . . . . less than $1–$10

Four-Spotted Trivia
Trivia quadripunctata, Gray. Pink with 1 to 4 brownish dots on both sides of the median furrow, this shell is about ¼ in. (6 mm) long. It is common in shallow water from Florida to the West Indies. . . . . $1–$5

Suffuse Trivia
Trivia suffusa, Gray. The pink shell usually has faint blotches, and the riblets are beaded at the median furrow. Less than ¼ in. (6 mm) long, it is common in shallow water from south Florida to the West Indies. . . . $1–$6

Simnia & Cyphoma Snails { Family :: Ovulidae }

The members of this family are glossy slender shells and live on sea whips and sea fans (*Gorgonia* sp.). Each species of *Cyphoma* has a characteristically colored and patterned mantle. It is believed that the colored simnias take on the color of the sea fans they inhabit.

Single-Toothed Simnia

Neosimnia uniplicata, Sowerby. This shell is commonly pink or purple, but can be white or yellow. The thin shell is ¾ in. (19 mm) long, and the long narrow aperture ends in a blunt point. This species is common from North Carolina to the West Indies. . . . . $2–$7

Flamingo Tongue

Cyphoma gibbosum, Linné. The solid shell has a dorsal hump across the center of the shell. It is about 1 in. (25 mm) long, white or yellowish with orange edges, and highly polished. This species is common from North Carolina to the West Indies.   . . . . less than $1–$2

McGinty's Cyphoma

Cyphoma mcgintyi, Pilsbry. The shell is about 1 in. (25 mm) long and is whitish with lavender tints. It is very similar to the flamingo tongue, but McGinty's cyphoma is more elongated and the hump is somewhat narrower. The shell is somewhat uncommon and is found in shallow water from the Florida Keys to the Bahamas. $4–$5

Moon Shells { Family :: Naticidae }

Extremely active carnivores, the moon snails feed on bivalves, eating as many as three or four clams a day. The snail digs out its prey from under the sand and pierces the shell with the radula and glandular acid, forming a hole through which the flesh is sucked up. The foot of the animal is so large that when extended, it often conceals the entire shell. The operculum can be either horny or calcareous.

Colorful Atlantic Natica

Natica canrena, Linné. The almost-round smooth shell is 1 to 2½ in. (25 to 64 mm) high and is yellowish white with spiral rows of brown spots, stripes, and zigzag markings. The limy operculum has numerous spiral grooves on the exterior side. Moderately common, the shell is found in sand in shallow water from North Carolina to Florida and to the West Indies. . . . . $2–$10

Livid Natica

Natica livida, Pfeiffer. This small glossy gray shell has a white band below the suture and darker spiral bands on the body whorl; the aperture is brown. The shell is $1/4$ to $3/4$ in. (6 to 19 mm) high and has a white calcareous operculum. Fairly common, it is found on sand flats in shallow water from southern Florida to the West Indies. . . . . less than $1–$4

Morocco Natica

Natica marochiensis, Gmelin. About $1/2$ to 1 in. (13 to 25 mm) high, the shell is grayish brown with a narrow white band below the suture and spiral bands of lightly defined reddish brown spots on the body whorl. The operculum is calcareous. The shell is common in sandy shallow water from southeast Florida to the West Indies. . . . . $2–$5

Shark's Eye

Polinices duplicatus, Say. The large shell, 2 to 3 in. (50 to 76 mm) high, is smooth, solid, and gray to tan in color. It is usually wider than it is high. The operculum is horny. A common shell, it is found on sand and mud flats in shallow water from Cape Cod, Massachusetts to Florida, the Gulf of Mexico, and Texas. . . . . . $1–$12

Brown Moon Shell

Polinices hepaticus, Röding. Previously classified as *Polinices brunneus*, Link. The thick shiny shell can be tan or orange brown and attains $1^{1}/2$ in. (38 mm) in height. The operculum is horny; the aperture is white. This uncommon shell is found in shallow to moderately shallow water from Florida to the West Indies. . . . . less than $1–$6

Milk Moon Shell

Polinices lacteus, Guilding. The shell is smooth, glossy, thick, and white with a thin yellowish periostracum. It is $1/2$ to $1^{1}/2$ in. (13 to 38 mm) high and has a thin reddish brown horny operculum. This species is common, found on sand in shallow water from North Carolina to Florida, the Gulf of Mexico, and Texas. . . . . $1–$3

Spotted Baby's Ear

Sinum maculatum, Say. This shell is differentiated from the common baby's ear by its more elevated profile and the weak yellowish brown spots on the white or buff shell. It is about $1^{1}/2$ in. (38 mm) across and has a rudimentary operculum. This uncommon shell is found in shallow water from North Carolina to Florida and the Gulf of Mexico. . . . . $1–$7

Common Atlantic Baby's Ear

Sinum perspecitivum, Say. This very flat shell is less than ½ in. (13 mm) high. It is white and 1½ in. (38 mm) in diameter. The body whorl accounts for more than 75% of the shell. It has a rudimentary operculum, a wide flaring aperture, and a very thin tan periostracum. It has an extremely large foot; live specimens have the shell virtually surrounded by the animal. This shell is common in sand in shallow water from Virginia to Florida and to the West Indies. . . . . less than $1–$3

Helmet & Bonnet Shells { Family :: Cassidae }

The shells in this family are thick, large, colorful, and characterized by having a large parietal shield. The aperture is long, the outer lip is usually thick and has teeth, and the inner lip generally has teeth, ridges, or bumps. Members of the genus *Cassis* have a horny oblong brown operculum, and they are used for carving as cameos. The genus *Phalium* has a fan-shaped operculum; in *Cypraecassis*, it is small and oval shaped or, in rare cases, absent completely. These species are found on sandy bottoms. The helmets feed on sea urchins and sand dollars.

Flame Helmet

Cassis flammea, Linné. The outer shell is yellow with brown marks and streaks. The parietal shield is rounded at the corners. The outer lip has well defined teeth without brown markings between them and the inner lip has wrinkles. The shell reaches a height of 3 to 6 in. (76 to 152 mm) and is highly polished. Fairly common, the flame helmet is found in shallow water from the Florida Keys to the West Indies and to Brazil. . . . . $4–$15

Queen Helmet or Emperor Helmet

Cassis madagascariensis, Lamarck. The largest member of the genus, this shell reaches a height of 14 in. (356 mm). It is white and has a large parietal shield. The outer lip is pale brown or salmon and is broad with elongated teeth and ridges. Teeth on the parietal shield have brownish black marks between them. Fairly common, the shell is found on sand in shallow water from southern Florida to the West Indies. . . . . $30–$70
13 in. (330 mm) $230

King Helmet

Cassis tuberosa, Linné. The tan or yellowish shell is mottled with brown and has brown between the fold on the inner lip and the teeth on the outer lip. The parietal shield is triangular, and the shell reaches a height of 4 to 9 in. (102 to 229 mm). This shell is the most common Atlantic helmet, found buried in sand in shallow water from North Carolina to the West Indies and Brazil. . . . . . . $12–$70

Reticulated Cowry Helmet

Cypraecassis testiculus, Linné. The large body whorl is brownish to pinkish orange with dark blotches and a crisscross pattern of lines on the surface. The parietal shield is oval and cream colored with some orange spots. The height is 1 to 3 in. (25 to 76 mm). Fairly common, this shell is found around reefs in shallow water from southeast Florida to Texas and to the West Indies and Brazil. . . . . $2–$12

Atlantic Wood Louse

Morum oniscus, Linné. This species is the smallest of the helmet shells, ⅝ to 1¼ in. (16 to 32 mm) high. It has irregular light-to-dark brown markings or is dark reddish brown overall with white flecks. It has small teeth on the thick outer lip. The shell is common, found under rocks and coral rubble in shallow water below the low-tide line from the Florida Keys to the West Indies and Brazil. . . . . $2–$6

Smooth Scotch Bonnet

Phalium cicatricosum, Gmelin. The pale yellow or white shell is marked with brown spots, similar in coloration to the Scotch bonnet, but the surface is smooth and shiny. It is about 2 in. (51 mm) high, and the parietal shield has pimplelike bumps. The shell is fairly common in moderately shallow water in its range from southern Florida to the West Indies and Brazil. . . . . $4–$10

Scotch Bonnet

Phalium granulatum, Born. The deep spiral grooves on the surface of the shell differentiate this species from the smooth Scotch bonnet. It is 2 to 4 in. (51 to 102 mm) high and yellowish or white with pale brown regular spots. The enlarged inner lip has numerous pimplelike bumps. The shell is common in the sand in shallow water from North Carolina to Florida and to the West Indies and Brazil. . . . . $3–$15

Royal Bonnet

Sconsia striata, Lamarck. The thick grayish shell has brown spots and fine revolving lines. It is about 2 in. (51 mm) high. The broad inner lip is polished; the outer lip is thick and has teeth within. This uncommon shell is found in deep water from Florida to the Gulf of Mexico, and to the West Indies and Brazil. . . . . $10–$35

Tritons are large rugged shells. They generally have teeth or folds on both the outer and inner lips of the aperture and have a long siphonal canal at the base. They have a high spire and a horny thick operculum. Most grow a horny or hairy periostracum, which protects the shell. Members of the family are carnivores, feeding on other snails, clams, and starfish, which they anesthesize with a glandular secretion and then insert the proboscis into the helpless prey to feed on the flesh. The large shells have been fashioned into horns since prehistoric times. Triton, the sea god of mythology, is portrayed with a trumpet made from a large seashell—thus "Triton's trumpet."

Triton's Trumpet

Charonia variegata, Lamarck. Formerly classified as *Charonia tritonis nobilis.* This strong solid shell is marked with patches of various colors—tan, brown, red, and purple. The aperture is orange, and the outer lip has pairs of small white teeth; there are whitish ridges on the inner lip. The shell is 10 to 15 in. (254 to 381 mm) high and has a thin translucent periostracum. Moderately common, it is found hiding in coral on reefs from southern Florida to the West Indies. . . . . $9–$85

The very similar Pacific species, *Charonia tritonis,* Linné, is found in Hawaii and reaches 18 in. (457 mm) in size. . . . . $12–$175

Dog-Head Triton

Cymatium caribbaeum, Clench and Turner. The pale yellow shell is irregularly blotched with gray and white, has heavy revolving ribs, and is 2 to 3 in. (51 to 76 mm) high. It is common, found in moderately shallow water from Florida to Texas and to the West Indies. . . . . . $5–$15

Angular Triton

Cymatium femorale, Linné. The large brownish shell, up to 7 in. (178 mm) high, is banded in darker shades, has prominent varices with white knobs, and has a white aperture. The periostracum flakes off when the shell is dry. This species is rare in Florida but common from the West Indies to Brazil; it is found in shallow water. . . . . $12–$35

Kreb's Triton

Cymatium krebsi, Mörch. The white or grayish shell is 2 to 3 in. (51 to 76 mm) high. It is not common; its range is from Florida to the West Indies. . . . . $3–$13

Knobbed Triton

Cymatium muricinum, Röding. This shell is yellowish, grayish white, or brown and is 1 to 2 in. (25 to 51 mm) high. The whorls may have many dense, beaded spiral cords and axial ribs that can form strong knobs, primarily on the body whorl. The thick outer lip is toothed and yellowish white. The shell is common, found on reefs from southeast Florida to the West Indies and Brazil. . . . . $2–$6

Gold-Mouthed Triton

Cymatium nicobaricum, Röding. Previously classified as *Cymatium chlorostomum*, Lamarck. The grayish or whitish shell, 2 to 3 in. (51 to 76 mm) high, is mottled with brown, and the surface is divided by crossing horizontal and vertical ribs. The aperture is orange or deep yellow, contrasting brightly with the white teeth. Found around reefs in shallow water, this species is fairly common from southeast Florida to the West Indies and Brazil. . . . . $2–$5

Neopolitan Triton

Cymatium parthenopeum, von Salis. Formerly listed as *Cymatium costatum*, Born. The height is 3 to 4 in. (76 to 102 mm), and the yellow-brown shell is lightly mottled with darker shades. Live specimens have a hairy periostracum. The aperture is rather large, and the outer lip is thick and knobby. The shell is uncommon, found in moderately shallow water from Florida to the West Indies. . . . . . .$3–$40

Atlantic Hairy Triton

Cymatium pileare, Linné. Previously classified as *Cymatium martinianum*, d'Orbigny. Named for the thick, brown, matted, and hairy periostracum of the living gastropod, the hairy triton is 3 to 5 in. (76 to 127 mm) high and is light brown with gray and white bands. Both lips on the aperture are wrinkled with small white teeth on a reddish background. Moderately common, this shell is found on reefs from South Carolina to Florida and to the West Indies, Brazil, and Hawaii. . . . . $1–$25

Poulsen's Triton

Cymatium poulseni, Mörch. The yellowish white to brown well-shouldered shell is 2 to 3 in. (51 to 76 mm) high and has a short acute spire and a wide aperture. Moderately common, it is found in deep water from Florida to Texas, the West Indies, and Venezuela. $2–$8

Tiger Triton

Cymatium tigrinus, Broderip. The shell is cream colored with brown mottlings and dark "tiger stripes" on both lips. The aperture is edged with light orange. The shell is 4 to 7 in. (102 to 178 mm) high. Adults have a flaring outer lip. This species is rare, found from the Gulf of California to Nicaragua and in the western Caribbean. .... $40–$75

Dwarf Hairy Triton

Cymatium vespaceum, Lamarck. This delicate and small shell, 1 to 1½ in. (25 to 38 mm) high, is yellowish white with brown and white varices. The small aperture is toothed on both lips, and the long canal is nearly closed. The shell is uncommon, found in moderately deep water from southern Florida to the West Indies and Brazil. .... $2–$8; $40

Atlantic Distorsio

Distorsio clathrata, Lamarck. This yellowish white shell is crosshatched with strong spiral and vertical ribs. It is 1 to 2 in. (25 to 51 mm) high and has a hairy periostracum. The aperture is strongly toothed and very distorted; the entire shell has a distorted appearance. Fairly common, it is found in sand in moderately deep water from Florida to the West Indies. .... $2–$10

Florida Distorsio

Distorsio mcgintyi, Emerson and Puffer. Also considered by some to be *Distorsio constricta mcgintyi*, a subspecies. This shell is tan and 1 to 1½ in. (25 to 38 mm) high, similar to the Atlantic distorsio but the surface has even coarser crosshatching. It has a hairy periostracum, and the outer lip is strongly toothed. Fairly common, it is found in moderately deep to deep water from Florida to the West Indies. .... $4–$8

Frog Shells { Family :: Bursidae }

Frog shells are carnivores, feeding on marine worms and bivalves. They have an oval-shaped aperture with a siphonal canal at both the top and the bottom. Members of this family have a horny operculum and a thick outer lip with small teeth.

California Frog Shell

Bursa californica, Hinds. This large shell is 1½ to 5 in. (38 to 127 mm) high and is yellowish white to brown, occasionally with brown spiral lines. The heavy thick shell has knobbed varices, and the aperture is white. The species is common, found in rocks in shallow water from Monterey, California, to Baja California. .... $10–$40

Gaudy Frog Shell

Bursa corrugata, Perry. This orange-brown shell is marked with darker shades. It is 2 to 3 in. (51 to 76 mm) high. The outer lip is broad and toothed. This uncommon shell is found in sand in moderately shallow water from southern Florida to the West Indies. . . . . $2–$30

Granular Frog Shell

Bursa granularis, Röding. This reddish brown shell is blotched with white and is 1 to 2 in. (25 to 51 mm) high. The yellow aperture has white teeth. The shell is common, found among rocks on reefs from southern Florida to the West Indies. . . . . $2–$10

Tun Shells { Family :: Tonnidae }

Tuns are medium- to large-size shells that are light but strong. They are carnivores that prey on sea cucumbers and bivalves. The long proboscis can be expanded to engulf the food whole. The shell is nearly round with a greatly enlarged body whorl. It has a large aperture with a toothless thin outer lip and lacks an operculum.

Giant Tun

Tonna galea, Linné. The average shell is about 6 in. (152 mm) high, but this light brown gastropod can attain a height of 10 in. (254 mm). The surface is encircled with grooves, the spire is very low, and the large aperture has a thickened outer lip in mature specimens. This shell is uncommon, found in sandy, moderately shallow offshore waters from North Carolina to Florida, the Gulf of Mexico, and Texas and to the West Indies. . . . $8–$35

Atlantic Partridge Tun

Tonna maculosa, Dillwyn. This shell can be pale to warm brown mottled with dark colors and crescent-shaped white marks, giving the surface the appearance of the feathers of a partridge. The shell is thin but strong and has spiral grooves. The aperture is tan with a thin sharp outer lip. This species is 2 to 5 in. (51 to 127 mm) high and is fairly common in sand in shallow water near coral reefs from southern Florida to the West Indies and to Brazil. . . . . $4–$18

There are many genera in this family; they are found worldwide in tropical and subtropical waters. Extremely variable in appearance, they are characterized by their strong, spiny shells. Typically, murex shells have strong spines and/or varices and a long siphonal canal. Generally found on rocks or reefs in shallow water, members of this family are carnivores—they prey on other snails, bivalves, worms, corals, barnacles, and invertebrates. The horny operculum is brown and thick.

Nuttall's Hornmouth

Ceratostoma nuttalli, Conrad. Yellowish gray or brown and often banded in white, the shell is 1 to 2 in. (25 to 51 mm) high. Adults have an apertural tooth. This shell is fairly common in moderately deep water from Monterey, California, to Baja California. . . . . $3–$20

Cabbage Murex

Hexaplex brassica, Lamarck. Previously classified as *Murex brassica*. At a height of 8 in. (203 mm), this shell is our largest member of this genus. It is whitish to pale reddish brown with 3 brown bands. The aperture and edges of the varices are pink. This rather common shell is found from the Gulf of California to Peru in moderately shallow water. . . . . $8–$24

Pink-Mouthed Murex

Hexaplex erythrostomus, Swainson. With a white aperture, it is known as *Murex bicolor*, Valenciennes. The rough surface of the shell is chalky white or pinkish white; the aperture is shiny and rosy pink. The height is 3 to 6 in. (76 to 152 mm). Fairly common but popular with collectors, the shell is found in moderately shallow water from the Gulf of California to Peru. . . . . $1–$13
White aperture . . . . $8–$15

Royal Murex

Hexaplex regius, Swainson. The aperture lips are bright pink darkening into deep brown on the parietal shield. The surface is mottled brown, and the shell reaches 5 to 6 in. (127 to 152 mm) in height. It is fairly common in moderately shallow water from the Gulf of California to Peru. . . . . $4–$30

Beau's Murex
Murex beaui, Fisher and Bernardi. The spiny varices often have thin wavy webs; the shell is creamy yellow or brownish, has a long canal, and is 3 to 4 in. (76 to 102 mm) high. It is uncommon and a prized collector's piece, found in deep water from southern Florida to the Gulf of Mexico and to the West Indies. .... $2–$70
Webbed .... $85–$695

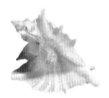

Bequaert's Murex
Murex bequaerti, Clench and Farfante. This white shell is 1 to 2½ in. (25 to 63 mm) high and has a sharp apex, a short closed canal, and a small aperture. It is rare, found in deep water from North Carolina to the Florida Keys and the Gulf of Mexico. .... $25–$350

West Indian Murex or Short-Frond Murex
Murex brevifrons, Lamarck. The shell is gray mottled with white and brown, and the fronds on the shoulders curve upwards. It is 3 to 6 in. (76 to 152 mm) high, and the fairly long siphonal canal is partially closed. This species is fairly common in moderately shallow water from southern Florida and the Florida Keys to the Gulf of Mexico and to the West Indies. .... $3–$30

Cabrit's Murex
Murex cabriti, Bernardi. The very long siphonal canal has long slender spines, which become shorter as they near the tip. The number and size of the spines varies, and they may even be absent. The pinkish tan shell can reach 3 in. (76 mm) in height. This uncommon shell is found in moderately deep water from Florida to the Gulf of Mexico and to the West Indies. .... $10–$45

Caillet's Murex
Murex cailleti, Petit. Yellowish with brown bands, this shell is 2 to 4 in. (50 to 102 mm) high. The siphonal canal is moderately long, closed, and curved. There usually are short spines on the varices. The shell is fairly common in deep water from southern Florida to the West Indies. .... $7–$13
White $23

Pitted Murex

Murex cellulosus, Conrad. This grayish or tan rough shell is about 1 in. (25 mm) high, and the varices at the tip of the closed canal form a fork. The inside of the round aperture is purplish. This shallow water species is common from North Carolina to the Gulf of Mexico and to the West Indies. . . . . $1–$5

Pitted Murex

Murex cellulosus leviculus, Dall. This shell is a subspecies of the previous shell, but it is not as common. It is found from off the eastern coast of Florida to the Gulf of Mexico. . . . . $2–$8

Gold-Mouthed Murex

Murex chrysostoma, Sowerby. This tan shell has a long siphonal canal and is 1½ to 3 in. (36 to 76 mm) long. It is fairly common from Florida to the West Indies. . . . . $4–$20

Lace Murex

Murex florifer, Reeve. This brownish shell has a pink apex and aperture and a rough surface with broad frondlike spines. It is 1 to 3 in. (25 to 76 mm) long. Juveniles are usually pink. The shell is common in shallow water from Florida to the West Indies. . . . . $4–$50

Giant Eastern Murex

Murex fulvescens, Sowerby. This large yellowish brown to whitish shell has a large body whorl and reaches 7 in. (178 mm) in height. It is common in sandy shallow water, where it feeds on the common oyster, from North Carolina to Florida and to Texas. . . . . $5–$65

McGinty's Murex

Murex mcgintyi, M. Smith. The shell is grayish white to tan, sometimes with brown markings on the varices. The 1 in. (25 mm) high shell has deep revolving ridges across the surface. The siphonal canal is broad, short, and partially closed. This rare shell is found in deep water from the Florida Keys to the West Indies. . . . . . . $12–$160

Apple Murex

Murex pomum, Gmelin. This species does not have spines. It is whitish or buff with brown bands and markings. It is 2 to 4½ in. (51 to 114 mm) high, and the short canal is nearly closed and curves backwards. This shell is common in shallow water from North Carolina to Florida and to the West Indies and Brazil. . . . . less than $2–25

Rose Murex

Murex recurvirostris rubidus, Baker. Also listed as *Murex rubidus.* This chunky shell is 1½ in. (38 mm) high. It has a long canal, which is almost closed, a round aperture, and a light yellow operculum. Its color varies: it can be cream, pink, orange, or red. The shell is common in shallow water from southern Florida to the West Indies. . . . . .$4–$20

Murex

Murex recurvirostris sallasi, Abbott and Rehder. Also listed as *Murex sallasi.* This cream-colored shell with weak brown bands has a pointed apex and a long siphonal canal. It is 1 to 2 in. (25 to 51 mm) high. The shell is rare, found in the Gulf of Mexico and the West Indies. . . $35–$45

Tryon's Murex

Murex tryoni, Hidalgo. This cream-colored shell is 1 to 1½ in. (25 to 38 mm) high and has a short spire and a long closed canal with spines. It is uncommon and is found in deep water from Florida to the West Indies. . . . . $35–$70

Woodring's Murex

Murex woodringi, Clench and Farfante. The grayish white shell occasionally has weak brown markings. It is 2 to 3 in. (51 to 76 mm) high and has a pointed apex. The long slender canal is partially closed, and the varices have short spines. This uncommon shell is found in deep water from the Gulf of Mexico to the West Indies. . . . . . . $9–$18

Black Murex

Muricanthus nigritus, Philippi. Also listed as *Murex nigritus.* This sturdy solid shell reaches a height of 8 in. (152 mm); the surface is white with encircling black ribs and spines. Juvenile specimens are almost completely white. The shell is common, found in moderately shallow water in the Gulf of California. . . . . $3–$28

Vitularia salebrosa, King and Broderip. This brownish shell with darker markings is solid and is 2 to 3 in. (51 to 76 mm) high. Its surface is rough, and there is a row of small knobs at the shoulder. It is common in moderately shallow water from California to Baja California. $1–$5

Drills { Family :: Muricidae }

These small rock dwellers drill holes in the shells of bivalves and, most importantly, oysters, which they favor. As a result, they destroy commercial shellfish beds.

Thick-Lipped Drill

Eupleura caudata, Say. This small solid shell varies in color from reddish brown to grayish white. It is ½ to 1 in. (13 to 25 mm) high and has a short, almost closed canal. The shell is common, found on oyster beds from Cape Cod, Massachusetts, to Florida. . . . . $2–$4

Eupleura muriciformis, Broderip. This gray shell is about 1¼ in. (32 mm) high and has a thick outer lip and a fairly long, nearly closed canal. It is common in shallow water from the Gulf of California to South America.   . $1–$3

Hexagonal Murex

Muricopsis oxytatus, M. Smith. This grayish shell, tinted with pink, is about 1¼ in. (32 mm) high. The surface is spiny, and the edge of the outer lip has frondlike projections. The shell is uncommon and is found in moderately shallow water from southern Florida to the West Indies. . . . . $3–$8

Muricopsis zeteki, Hertlein and Strong. This species has a gray shell with brown spines and is less than 1 in. (25 mm) high. It has a serrated thin outer lip. The shell is common, found in moderately shallow water in the Gulf of California. . . . . $1–$5

False Drill Shell

Pseudoneptunea multangula, Philippi. The color varies from cream with brown flecks to, less commonly, brown or orange. The shell is 1 to 1¼ in. (25 to 32 mm) high and has a short canal and thin outer lip. It is uncommon, found in moderately shallow water from North Carolina to Florida and Texas and to the West Indies. . . $2–$10

33

Tampa Drill Shell

Urosalpinx tampaensis, Conrad. This rugged grayish brown shell is mottled with white and is ½ to 1 in. (13 to 25 mm) high. It is destructive to oyster beds but not as common as *U. cinerea,* the Atlantic oyster drill, which is similar to this species but much more numerous and can be devastating to commercial oyster beds. This shell is found in mud flats in western Florida. .... $1–$2

Rock Shells & Dogwinkles
{ Family :: Muricidae; also classified in Thaididae }

Members of this family are carnivores and have stout shells with a large body whorl, a wide aperture, and a short spire. Most species live on rocks in intertidal areas, though some live in deeper quiet water; the latter generally have more spines. Live shells exude a green, red, or purple secretion.

Wide-Mouthed Rock Shell

Purpura patula, Linné. A large body whorl makes up most of the rough solid shell in this species, which is 2 to 3 ½ in. (51 to 89 mm) high. The surface is grayish green or brown with prominent nodules in young specimens; the interior is salmon colored. This shell is common in intertidal waters on rocks from Florida to the West Indies. .... $1–$3

Deltoid Rock Shell

Thais deltoidea, Lamarck. This stocky gray or white shell with brown and violet blotches has three spiral rows of knobs on the body whorl, with the two rows on the shoulders forming blunt spines. It is 1 to 2 in. (25 to 51 mm) high. The shell is common and found among rocks, often heavily encrusted, in intertidal areas from Florida to the West Indies. .... $1–$3

Florida Rock Shell

Thais haemastoma floridana, Conrad. This cream or orange shell with brown marks is 2 to 3 in. (51 to 76 mm) high and has a thick outer lip and a short canal and flesh-colored aperture. This common shell is found in intertidal areas on oyster beds from North Carolina to Florida and the Gulf of Mexico and to the West Indies and Brazil. .... $1–$4

Channeled Dogwinkle

Nucella canaliculata, Duclos. Also listed as *Thais canaliculata*. The white or grayish to brown shell has a prominent spire and a deep suture. It is 1 to 1½ in. (25 to 38 mm) high. This shell is common, found in rock crevices in intertidal areas from Alaska to Monterey, California.
. . . . $1–$3

Frilled Dogwinkle

Nucella lamellosa, Gmelin. Also listed as *Thais lamellosa*. The form and color of the shell is variable: from white to light brown, occasionally with brown bands, and it can be smooth or sculptured. It is 1 to 3¼ in. (25 to 83 mm) high. The outer lip is white and broadly flared. This shell is common in protected rock crevices from the intertidal area to below the low-tide line from Alaska to California.
. . . . $2–$8

Coral Shells
{ Family :: Maagilidae; also classified in Coralliophilidae }

These small thick shells may be sculptured with spiral series of spines or be smooth. They can be white, yellow, or pink and, in some cases, have a bright purple aperture. Coral shells are carnivores and live with stony and soft corals. A few species live among anemones.

Short Coral Shell

Coralliophila abbreviata, Lamarck. This white to grayish white thick shell has a large body whorl, a low spire, and a deep canal, which is open. The outer lip is strongly toothed. The shell is about 1 in. (25 mm) high, and the aperture is pink or violet. The shell is common at bases of stony corals and sea fans from Florida to the West Indies and Brazil. . . . . $2–$6

Coralliophila costata, Blainville. This sturdy shell is gray with a purple aperture and is about 1 in. (25 mm) high. The outer lip is somewhat thickened. Fairly common, the shell is found on coral from the Gulf of California to Panama. . . . . $6–$7

Coralliophila deburghiae, Reeve. This shell is light gray to tan and has a sculptured surface with knobs at the sutures. It is 1 to 1½ in. (25 to 38 mm) high. This uncommon shell is found on corals in Florida and the Gulf of Mexico. $10

Dove Shells { Family :: Columbellidae }

Members of this family are small shells that can be ovate to elongate in shape. They can be smooth or sculptured and have high pointed or low broad spires. They feed on algae.

Common Dove Shell
Columbella mercatoria, Linné. Extremely variable in color, the shell is usually white with brown but may be solid white or spotted with yellow or orange. The solid shell is only ½ in. (13 mm) high and has many revolving grooves. It is common in shallow water from Florida to the West Indies. . . . . $1–$2

Nassas & Dog Whelks { Family :: Nassariidae }

Most species of these small carnivorous snails are scavengers, but some prey on oysters and thin-shelled mollusks. Their surface may be smooth or heavily sculptured, the spire is pointed, and the short canal is open.

Variable Nassa
Nassarius consensus, Ravenel. About ½ in. (13 mm) high, the shell is light brown with white markings. It is common, found in shallow water from Florida to the West Indies. . . . . less than $1–$2

Channeled Dog Whelk
Nassarius fossatus, Gould. Up to 1¾ in. (45 mm) high, this whelk is the largest west coast member of the species. It has a shiny yellowish tan shell with a bright orange interior, a high spire, and fine spiral lines. It is common in shallow water from British Columbia to Baja California. . . . . $2–$7

Nassarius hotessieri, d'Orbigny. This small gray shell is ½ to 1 in. (6 to 13 mm) high and has axial ribs along each whorl. It is common in shallow water in Florida and the Gulf of Mexico. . . . . $1–$3

Small Whelks, Cantharus Shells, Dwarf Tritons, & Pisa Shell { Family :: Buccinum }

Members of this family are carnivores; they are scavengers and also actively prey on bivalves by means of a long proboscis. All species have a well defined canal and horny operculum. The surface of the shell may be smooth or have a spiral or axial sculpture or a combination.

Common Northern Whelk

Buccinum undatum, Linné. Yellowish white to yellow brown in color, live specimens have a light brown periostracum. Their surface has numerous weak spiral cords. The shell is 3 to 4 in. (76 to 102 mm) high and is very common on rocks in shallow to moderately deep water from the Arctic Ocean to New Jersey and also to Europe. This snail is eaten in some parts of Europe. . . . $3–$12
Sinistral $720

Gaudy Cantharus

Cantharus auritula, Link. This stout solid shell, ¾ to 1¼ in. (19 to 32 mm) high, is mottled with brown, gray, and black and has a short canal and thick outer lip. The shell is common, found in shallow water from southern Florida to the West Indies. . . . . $1–$2

Cancellate Cantharus

Cantharus cancellaria, Conrad. The reddish brown shell is marked with white mottlings and is sculptured both spirally and axially. It is ¾ to 1¼ in. (19 to 32 mm) high and is elongated, with a thick outer lip. It is common in shallow water from Florida to Texas. . . . . . less than $1–$5

Cantharus ringens, Reeve. The surface of this grayish brown shell is sculptured with prominent spiral cords. The shell is about 1 in. (25 mm) high, and its toothed outer lip is thickened. It is common from the Gulf of California to Central America. . . . . $2–$3

Tinted Cantharus

Cantharus tinctus, Conrad. This solid shell is about 1 in. (25 mm) high. Its color is variable, and it has a very short canal, a thick outer lip, and a tooth at the upper end of the aperture. The shell is common, found in weeds in the intertidal zone from North Carolina to Florida and Texas and to the West Indies. . . . . $1–$2

Arrow Dwarf Triton
Colubraria lanceolata, Menke. The surface of this slender gray shell with orange-brown blotches has many fine vertical lines. The shell is about 1 in. (25 mm) high and is common, found under rocks in shallow to moderately deep water from North Carolina to Florida and the West Indies. .... $3–$8

Colubraria testacea, Mörch. The shell is primarily brown but with lighter bands and is ½ to 1½ in. (13 to 38 mm) high. The surface has fine lines of spiral cords. This shell is uncommon and is found from Florida to the West Indies. .... $5–$12

New England Neptune or Ten-Ridged Whelk
Neptunea decemcostata, Say. This shell is gray with prominent reddish brown ridges and a white aperture. It is 3 to 4 in. (76 to 102 mm) high. This species is common, but it is not generally found in good condition on shore. These shells are frequently caught in fishermen's nets and lobster traps. They are found on rocky bottoms in moderately shallow water from Nova Scotia to Massachusetts.
.... $4–$20
Color variant .... $40–$50

Pisa Shell
Pisania pusio, Linné. This smooth polished shell is purplish brown, marked with irregular dark and light spots, and about 1½ in. (38 mm) high. Its spire is well developed, and the apex is pointed. The shell is common in moderately shallow water and on reefs from southern Florida to the West Indies. .... $1–$3

Whelks & Crown Conchs { Family :: Melongenidae }

Shallow-water species in this family are moderately large to large and have a solid shell, a large body whorl, and a horny oval operculum, which is pointed at one end. They are primarily carnivores; they are either scavengers or they prey on live tulip snails and oysters. Their shell sculpture is varied.

Channeled Whelk
Busycon canaliculatum, Linné. This pear-shaped shell is 3½ to 7½ in. (89 to 190 mm) high. It has a broad, deeply channeled suture and a large yellow-brown aperture. The shell is gray to cream colored, covered with a thick hairy gray periostracum. This common shell is found in sand and mud in the intertidal zone to just below the low-tide line from Massachusetts to northern Florida; it was also introduced in California. As late as 1925, this species was sold as food in Boston. .... $2–$5

Kiener's Whelk

Busycon carica eliceans, Montfort. This heavy shell has strong spines on a large body whorl and is 4 to 9 in. (102 to 229 mm) high. It has a long open canal. The surface is grayish white to grayish brown, and the aperture is reddish orange. The shell is very similar to the knobbed whelk, *Busycon carica,* Gmelin, except Kiener's whelk is heavier, has heavier spines on the body whorl, and has a spiral swelling around the lower part of the body whorl. Kiener's whelk is common, found in shallow water from North Carolina to Florida. . . . . $5–$12

The knobbed whelk is also common in shallow water, but its range extends from Massachusetts to Florida. $3–$8

Turnip Whelk

Busycon coarctatum, Sowerby. This species has a long open canal and a short spire with the sutures bearing short brown sharp spines. The grayish surface is streaked vertically with brownish purple marks. Its aperture is yellow orange, and it may attain a height of 6 in. (152 mm). This uncommon shell is found in moderately shallow water in the Gulf of Mexico. . . . . $10–$28

Lightning Whelk

Busycon contrarium, Conrad. This large tan to grayish white shell is 2½ to 16 in. (64 to 406 mm) high and has fine reddish brown axial lines on the surface. It is a sinistral shell (rarely, dextral) with a large body whorl that narrows to a long open canal. The aperture is white. The shell is common in sand from the low-tide line to shallow water; it is found from North Carolina to Florida and Texas. . . . . $1–$15
Right-handed (dextral) $120
300 mm+ $28

dextral

Pear Whelk

Busycon spiratum, Lamarck. Previously classified as *Busycon pyrum,* Dillwyn. This pear-shaped shell usually has smooth rounded shoulders and a long siphonal canal. It is flesh colored, streaked with reddish brown, and is 3 to 5 in. (76 to 127 mm) high. The tan periostracum is fuzzy. The shell is common in shallow water from North Carolina to Florida and the Gulf states. . . . . . . $4–$5

Florida Crown Conch

Melongena corona, Gmelin. This brown shell is banded with white, blue, and yellow. It is 1 to 8 in. (25 to 203 mm) high and has a clawlike operculum. The presence of spines varies greatly, with some forms being spineless (as a result of dietary deficiency), other forms with one or more rows of spines on the shoulders, and still others, rarely, with multiple spines. The shell is primarily a scavenger but will attack live bivalves. It is common in mud or muddy sand in shallow water from Florida to the Gulf of Mexico and Alabama and to Mexico. less than $1–$3

West Indian Crown Conch or Brown Crown Conch

Melongena melongena, Linné. This shell is whitish with brownish purple bands, which in some specimens cover most of the shell. It is 2 to 7 in. (51 to 178 mm) high and has a short spire with vertical ribs. The body whorl may be smooth or have 2 or 3 rows of sharp spines on the periphery and a row of spines near the base. It feeds on mollusks, primarily bivalves, including oysters. It is found in mud and sand in brackish water at mouths of bays or lagoons in the West Indies. . . . . $4–$15

Tulip Shells, Horse Conch, & Spindle Shells
{ Family :: Fasciolariidae }

These snails are spindle shaped and have a strong thick shell, an elongated spire, and a rather long siphonal canal. The horny operculum is oval shaped and completely covers the opening when the animal is withdrawn. These shells are predators with slow deliberate movement, feeding on mollusks and, in some cases, sea worms and barnacles.

Branham's Tulip

Fasciolaria branhamae, Rehder and Abbott. Also listed as subspecies, *Fasciolaria hunteria branhamae*. The shell is 3 to 5 in. (76 to 127 mm) high, which makes it larger than *F. hunteria*, and it also has a longer siphonal canal. The shell is whitish with brown-colored spiral lines. It is fairly common but is found in deep water in the Gulf of Mexico. . . . . $2–$10

Banded Tulip

Fasciolaria hunteria, Perry. One color variation of this tan shell with narrow brown spiral lines has bluish gray vertical cloudings; the other variation has similar orange markings. It is 2 to 4 in. (51 to 102 mm) high, and the surface is smooth. A common species, the shell is found in shallow water in sandy mud and weeds from North Carolina to Florida and the Gulf of Mexico. . . . . less than $1–$5
Albino $125

True Tulip

Fasciolaria tulipa, Linné. The color of this shell is variable—usually grayish green or grayish white with brownish or orange axial splotches. It is 2 to 9 in. (51 to 229 mm) high and preys on other gastropods and bivalves but favors large snails such as pear whelks, banded tulips, and small queen conchs. This common shell is found on sand and mud from the intertidal zone to moderately shallow water from North Carolina to Florida and Texas and to the West Indies. . . . . $2–$15
180 mm+ $20

Short-Tailed Latirus

Latirus brevicaudatus, Reeve. The knobby whorls of this shell have well-defined sutures. The shell is light brown with darker encircling lines and is 1 to 2 in. (25 to 51 mm) high. Moderately common, it is found in shallow water in the Florida Keys and the West Indies. $2–$13

Brown-Lined Latirus

Latirus infundibulum, Gmelin. This elongated tan shell has many orange-brown spiral cords. It is about 2 in. (51 mm) high and has a narrow long canal and 2 or 3 pleats on the inner lip. It is found in moderately shallow water from southern Florida (uncommon) to the West Indies.
. . . . $3–$15

McGinty's Latirus

Latirus mcgintyi, Pilsbry. This heavy solid yellowish shell has brown markings between strong, rounded vertical ribs and is ½ to 2½ in. (13 to 63 mm) high. The shell is uncommon, and it is found in moderately shallow water near reefs in southern Florida. . . . . $2–$8

Chestnut Latirus

Leucozonia nassa, Gmelin. This heavy chestnut brown shell has 9 to 10 pronounced knobs on the shoulders of the lower whorls and a short open canal. It is 1 to 2 in. (25 to 51 mm) high. A common species, it is found under rocks or wet sand on reefs from the intertidal zone to below the low-tide line. Its range is from Florida to Texas and to the West Indies. $2–$12

White-Spotted Latirus

Leucozonia ocellata, Gmelin. This small, 1 in. (25 mm), heavy brown shell has whitish knobs at the periphery of the whorls and small white spots at the base of the shell. The apex is white in mature specimens. This shell is common, found in the intertidal area from Florida to the West Indies. . . . . $2–$5

Opeatostoma pseudodon, Burrow. The surface of this grayish white shell has dark brown revolving lines. The base of the aperture has a long needlelike tooth, and the shell is 2½ in. (63 mm) high. It is common, found in moderately shallow water from the Gulf of California to Peru.
. . . . $2–$10

Florida Horse Conch

Pleuroploca gigantea, Kiener. This very large heavy shell can reach 24 in. (610 mm) in height. The immature specimens are orange; older shells are grayish white to salmon and brown with a brown flaky periostracum; rarely, some shells are albinos. The whorls on the spire have triangular knobs, and the long open canal is slightly twisted. The horse conch is one of the largest gastropods in the world. It feeds primarily on other large snails—tulip shells, lightning whelks, and lace murex—and on pen shells. The horse conch prevents its prey from closing the aperture by holding the victim's operculum. It then inserts its proboscis and eats the soft parts of the animal. This shell is a common species, but large shells are becoming rare due to overcollecting. It is found in sand and mud from the low-tide line to moderately shallow water from North Carolina to Florida, Texas, and Mexico.
Large . . . . $35–$125
Large albino $200

Pleuroploca reevei, Philippi. This shell is similar to the Florida Horse Conch, except *P. reevei* does not have knobs on the spire whorls. The shell is large, from 8 to 18 in. (203 to 457 mm) high; some regard this shell as merely another knobless form of the Florida horse conch. Its range is limited to Florida. . . . . $2–$25

Coue's Spindle

Fusinus couei, Petit. This white tall shell of 4 in. (102 mm) has distinct sutures, a small aperture, and a long canal, which is nearly closed. It is common, found in deep water in the Gulf of Mexico. . . . . $2–$20

Fusinus dupetitthouarsi, Kiener. White or cream colored, the shell has a greenish yellow periostracum. It is 6 to 10 in. (152 to 254 mm) high, and the open canal is very long. The shell is common in moderately shallow water in the Gulf of California. . . . . $3–$22

Ornamented Spindle

Fusinus eucosmius, Dall. The color of this shell can vary from pure white to orange white. The periostracum is thick and yellowish. The spire is sharply pointed, the canal is long and thin, and the shell is 2 ½ in. (64 mm) high. Fairly common, this shell is found in moderately deep water in the Gulf of Mexico. .... $4–$12

Fusinus halistrepus, Dall. This slender white shell is 1½ in. (38 mm) long. It is uncommon and is found in the Gulf of Mexico. .... $8–$12

Fusinus helenae, Bartsch. This elongated white shell is 1½ in. (38 mm) long and has a long canal. The shell is uncommon; it is found in the Gulf of Mexico. . $7–$20

Turnip Spindle

Fusinus timessus, Dall. This rather chunky shell is 3 in. (76 mm) high and has a deep suture and a long, nearly closed canal. The shell is white and is occasionally tinted with yellow orange. It is uncommon, found in deep water in the Gulf of Mexico. .... $3–$15

Olive Shells { Family :: Olividae }

These elongated cylindrical shells are smooth and glossy, because the mantle and foot in the living snail usually covers and protects the shell. They have a large body whorl and a small conical spire. Those in the genus *Oliva* usually lack an operculum, while other genera may have them. They are carnivores, preying on bivalves and crabs, which they enclose in the foot. They then burrow into the sand to digest the catch.

Caribbean Olive

Oliva caribaeensis, Dall and Simpson. This shell is generally a grayish purple with a purplish aperture, but some varieties are reddish brown with a light aperture. The shiny smooth surface also has darker lines and white specks. It is 1½ in. (38 mm) high and is common in the intertidal zone in the West Indies. .... $2–$3

Oliva incrassata, Lightfoot. The solid shell of about 2 in. (51 mm) high has a wider aperture than most olives, and the pinkish gray surface is flecked and streaked with lavender and gray. The inner lip is bright pink in fresh specimens. The shell is common except for an occasional rare yellow unmarked specimen; it is found from the Gulf of California to Peru. .... $2–$13
Corded .... $40–$50

Tent Olive
Oliva porphyria, Linné. This 4 in. (102 mm) shell is the largest of our olives. It is grayish with a network of thin brown zigzag lines, which in some areas are dense enough to form brown patches. Fairly common, it is found in shallow water in the Gulf of California. Rare specimens are corded. . . . . $10–$100

Netted Olive
Oliva reticularis, Lamarck. This white or gray shell has a shiny surface and is marked with a pattern of purplish brown netlike lines. This common species is 1½ to 2 in. (38 to 51 mm) high; it is found in sand in shallow to moderately shallow water from southern Florida to the West Indies. . . . . $1–$5

Oliva reticularis bollingi, Clench. This subspecies of netted olive is 1½ to 2 in. (38 to 51 mm) high. It is cream colored with indistinct markings and is moderately common in sand in deep water from southern Florida to the Bahamas. . . . . $2–$4

Oliva reticularis greenwayi, Clench. This shell is another subspecies, marked with dark reddish brown bands. It is found in southern Florida and the Bahamas. The shell is moderately common and is 1½ to 2 in. (38 to 51 mm) high. It is found in sand. $2–$4

Oliva reticularis olorinella, Duclos. The color of this subspecies varies from bluish gray to grayish. There is also a rare albino specimen. The shell is common except for the albino and is 1½ to 2 in. (38 to 51 mm) high. It is found in the Bahamas and throughout the West Indies. $3–$12

Lettered Olive
Oliva sayana, Ravenel. This strong shell is highly polished. It is cream to gray with the surface heavily marked in reddish brown zigzag markings and is 2 to 2¾ in. (51 to 70 mm) high. This common species is usually found buried in sand with only the siphon sticking out. Its range is from North Carolina to Florida and Texas and to the West Indies and Brazil. . . . . $2–$20
Albino $30

Purple Dwarf Olive

Olivella biplicata, Sowerby. This grayish shell (sometimes almost white) has a purplish band at the base, and the outer lip is purplish within. Immature and young specimens are tinted with purple. This common species is $\frac{1}{2}$ to 1 in. (13 to 38 mm) high and is found on sand from the intertidal zone to moderately deep water from Vancouver Island, B.C., to Baja California. .... $2–$5

West Indian Dwarf Olive

Olivella nivea, Gmelin. This small shell is $\frac{1}{2}$ to 1 in. (13 to 25 mm) high. The shiny surface is white with orange-brown markings. It is common, found in the intertidal zone to moderately deep water from Florida to the West Indies. .... $1–$5

Miter Shells { Family :: Mitridae }

The shape of these shells varies from ovate to elongate. The surface usually has spiral cords and in some cases may have axial ribs or be smooth without any sculpture. The shells are found in sand or coral rubble, where these carnivores feed by means of a long proboscis on marine worms and occasionally mollusks. The operculum is absent, but they have a thin periostracum and a sharply pointed spire.

Barbados Miter

Mitra barbadensis, Gmelin. The elongated shell is tan with white marks. The surface has weak spiral cords, and the aperture is long and narrow. This common shell is 1 to $1\frac{1}{2}$ in. (25 to 38 mm) high and is found in intertidal areas around open oceanic reefs from southern Florida to the West Indies. .... $1–$6

Royal Florida Miter

Mitra florida, Gould. The smooth white shell has many spiral rows of yellowish brown dots and is $1\frac{1}{2}$ to 2 in. (38 to 51 mm) high. It is rare, found in moderately shallow water on sand around coral reefs from southern Florida to the West Indies. .... $15–$50

Chank Shells
{ Family :: Xanidae; also classified in Turbinellidae }

Members of this family range in size from ¼ to 14 in. (13 to 356 mm) high. They have a fairly long siphonal canal and are carnivores. They are found in tropical and subtropical water from just below the low-tide line to very deep water.

Chank Shell or Lamp Shell
Xancus angulatus, Lightfoot. Previously classified as *Turbinella scolymus,* Gmelin; also classified as *Turbinella angulata,* Lightfoot. This yellowish white shell is heavy and has prominent knobs on the shoulders. It is 5 to 14 in. (127 to 356 mm) high and has a rounded apex, a horny clawlike operculum, and a brown periostracum. This carnivorous species feeds on tube worms and bivalves. This uncommon shell is found in shallow water on sand or rubble from southern Florida to the West Indies. . . . . $5–$8
More than 15 in. (400 mm) . . . . $35–$50

Vase Shells { Family :: Vasidae }

Representatives of this family can be heavy top shaped or elongated ovate with a narrow base, or they can be spindle shaped with a long slender canal. They are found in sand near reefs and are carnivores, feeding on bivalves and sea worms. Their operculum is clawlike, and they usually have a heavy periostracum.

Spiny Vase Shell
Vasum capitellus, Linné. This vase-shaped yellowish brown shell is 2 to 3 in. (51 to 76 mm) high, and the surface has strongly rounded vertical ribs, which produce heavy spines on the shoulders. The base of the body whorl has two rows of spines. The shell is fairly common in shallow water in the West Indies. . . . . $2–$10

Caribbean Vase Shell
Vasum muricatum, Born. This large heavy vase-shaped shell is 2½ to 5 in. (64 to 127 mm) high, yellowish white in color, and covered with a brown periostracum. The last spire whorls have strongly angled knobs at the periphery, and the wide body whorl has 9 to 10 strong triangular-shaped knobs at the periphery, often with smaller knobs below. There are 2 to 4 rows of triangular knobs on the ridges near the base. This shell is fairly common in shallow water from southern Florida to the West Indies. . . . . $1–$8

Harp Shells { Family :: Harpidae }

This family is characterized by the large flaring apertures and vertical ribbing. The shells are ornate. They have no operculum and are primarily Indo-Pacific, with but a single species found off North America.

Harp Shell

Harpa crenata, Swainson. This pale shell with purplish brown ribs and spots on the ribs has brown and violet chevronlike marks in the spaces between the ribs. Most of the shell consists of the enlarged body whorl; the spire is short and pointed; the aperture flares. The shell is 2 to 3 in. (51 to 76 mm) high. It is fairly common, found in moderately shallow water in the Gulf of California.
. . . . $3–$8
80 mm+ . . . . $15–$20

Volutes { Family :: Volutidae }

The shells in this family are among the most costly specimens to buy. These colorful prized shells range from elongated to broadly oval, and most volutes have a bulbous nuclear whorl at the apex. Adults are generally smooth, but they can occasionally have spines or knobs near the upper part of the body whorl. Volutes may or may not have an operculum. They are carnivores and feed on small marine invertebrates.

Scaphella cuba, Clench. Also listed as *Voluta cuba*. Cream or white with spiral rows of reddish brown spots, this rare species reaches a height of 2 in. (51 mm). Its range includes the north coast of Cuba and the Florida Straits. $60

Dohrn's Volute

Scaphella dohrni, Sowerby. Also listed as *Voluta dohrni*. This slender gray or white shell is marked with spiral rows of squarish brown spots. It has a moderately tall spire and is 2 to 4 in. (51 to 102 mm) high. This rare shell is found in deep water off the southern half of Florida.
. . . . $10–$100

Dubious Volute

Scaphella dubia, Broderip. Also listed as *Voluta dubia*. This shell is slender and is tan to pinkish with brown spots, but the markings are fewer than on Dohrn's volute. It is 3 to 4 in. (76 to 102 mm) high, and there are vertical ribs on the upper whorls. This uncommon shell is found in deep water off southern Florida and in the Gulf of Mexico. . . . . $15–$120; $450

Scaphella georgiana, Clench. Also listed as *Voluta georgiana.* This tan shell reaches a height of 3 to 4 in. (76 to 102 mm). The brown spots on the surface are less dense and smaller than in the other spotted volutes. This species is rare, found from Georgia to the east coast of Florida. .... $30–$125; $350

Gould's Volute

Scaphella gouldiana, Dall. Also listed as *Voluta gouldiana.* This yellowish gray shell may have broad brown spiral bands, or occasionally it may be mostly white. Its surface is sculptured with short ribs at the shoulders. It reaches 2 to 3 in. (51 to 76 mm) in height. This uncommon shell is found in deep water from North Carolina to Florida and the West Indies. .... $20–$150
Albino. $250

Junonia

Scaphella junonia, Shaw. This rather large shell, 3 to 6 in. (76 to 152 mm) high, is creamy white with rows of squarish spots, which are dark brown or reddish orange. It is very popular with collectors but not as rare as it once was believed to be, since it is found by shrimp fishermen regularly. There is no operculum. This uncommon shell is found in moderately deep water from North Carolina to Florida and the Gulf of Mexico. .... $5–$150

Kiener's Volute

Scaphella kieneri, Clench. Also listed as *Voluta kieneri* and *Auriniopsis kieneri.* This large slender shell is tan and has rectangular-shaped spots, which are dark brown or black in spiral rows around the shell. The shell is 5 to 8 in. (127 to 203 mm) high, and while considered rare at one time, it has become more available as a by-product of the shrimp fishing industry. It is fairly common in deep water in the Gulf of Mexico. .... $15–$350

Music Volute

Voluta musica, Linné. This grayish white or pinkish shell is marked with spots and lines resembling the staff and notes of musical notation. It is thick shelled and oval shaped. The shell is 2 to 3½ in. (51 to 89 mm) high and has a small horny operculum. Fairly common, it is found in coral sand in shallow water in the West Indies. .... $7–$65

Nutmegs { Family :: Cancellariidae }

These oval-shaped shells have a broad aperture ending in a short canal and are both spirally and axially sculptured. They lack an operculum, but they can seal the shell opening with a mixture of sand and mucus. Nutmegs are carnivores and can be found in both shallow and fairly deep water.

Nutmeg

Cancellaria conradiana, Dall. Most macologists believe this shell is really only a variation of the common nutmeg, *C. reticulata.* It is 1 to 1½ in. (25 to 38 mm) high and oval shaped but elongated slightly. It has brownish orange bands on a white shell. The shell is sculptured in both directions. It is common in shallow water from North Carolina to both coasts of Florida. . . . . less than $1–$3

Common Nutmeg

Cancellaria reticulata, Linné. Broader and more heavily colored than *C. conradiana,* this shell is 1 to 1½ in. (25 to 38 mm) high and is cream or gray with orange-brown bands. The sculpture consists of both spiral cords and weak axial ribs. It is common in sand in shallow water from North Carolina to Florida and Texas. . . . . $2–$5

Adele's Nutmeg

Cancellaria reticulata adelae, Pilsbry. This subspecies of the common nutmeg is 1 to 1½ in. (25 to 38 mm) high. It has a cream-colored shell marked with orange-brown bands, and the body whorl is smooth. This snail is rare, found in shallow water in the Florida Keys. . . . . $2–$5

Philippi's Nutmeg

Trigonostoma tenerum, Philippi. About 1 in. (25 mm) high, this thin shell has four whorls, broad shoulders, and blunt beads covering the surface. It is pale yellow orange. The shell is uncommon and is found in moderately shallow water from southern Florida to the West Indies.
. . . . $6–$7

Margin shells, as they are also called, are small, shiny, and usually colorful shells, and most have a low spire. They have no operculum. Their aperture is narrow, and the outer lip has a thick margin, thus the common name. These snails have a large foot and mantle, the latter often covering most of the shell. They are carnivores and live in sand on reefs amid marine growth or under rocks.

Common Atlantic Margin Shell
Prunum apicinum, Menke. This solid shell is ½ in. (13 mm) high and has a low spire and an enlarged body whorl. The glossy surface is usually bright yellow to brownish orange, but a gray variety is found in the Florida Keys. There are 2 or 3 brownish spots on the outer lip. Rare specimens are sinistral. This shell is a very common, found in shallow water from North Carolina to Florida and the Gulf of Mexico and to the West Indies.   less than $1–$2
Sinistral $25

Orange Marginella
Prunum carneum, Storer. The shiny orange body whorl of this shell has white bands. The shell is ¾ in. (19 mm) high and has a thickened rolled outer lip. It is uncommon, found on coral reefs from below the low-tide line to moderately shallow water. . . . . $3–$20

White-Spotted Marginella
Prunum guttatum, Dillwyn. The shiny cream-colored shell has three pinkish gray bands on the body whorl and is covered with irregular white flecks. The outer lip is smooth white with brown spots. It is ¾ in. (19 mm) high, fairly common, and found in shallow water in coral sand from southern Florida to the West Indies. . . . . . $1–$4

Cone Shells { Family :: Conidae }

These shells are easily recognizable by their conic shape, which the common name describes. The members of this family are generally solid and have vividly colored shells decorated in a great variety of patterns. They are among the favorites of shell collectors, and some specimens sell for thousands of dollars. The spire varies from flattened to elevated. The surface can be smooth or have cords. The operculum is horny and elongated but is only one-fifth the length of the opening. Many species have a heavy periostracum, which must be removed to display the colors of the shell. Cones have a harpoon-shaped radula that, along with a neurotoxic venom, is injected by the proboscis into the victim to aid in its capture. Cone shells live in rocks and coral and are active at night, especially at low tide, feeding on worms, other mollusks, and, in the case of some Indo-Pacific species, occasionally on fish. Live cone shells should be handled carefully. Even though none of the species in our range are dangerous, they can inflict a painful and irritating sting. Only a few Indo-Pacific species are known to inflict fatal wounds on humans.

Austin's Cone

Conus austini, Rehder and Abbott. The whitish shell is 1 to 2½ in. (25 to 64 mm) high and has a surface sculpture of spiral cords crossing weak vertical lines. It has a high spire with a pointed apex. Found in moderately deep water from the Florida Keys to the West Indies, it was once considered fairly rare but is now often found by shrimp fishermen. . . . . $10–$50

California Cone

Conus californicus, Reeve. This yellowish brown shell is covered by a reddish brown periostracum, has a low spire, and is ¾ to 1½ in. (19 to 38 mm) high. This cone preys on a great variety of other living gastropods. It is fairly common, found in sand and gravel from the low-tide line to moderately deep water from San Francisco, California, to southern Baja California. . . . . $1–$10

Clark's Cone

Conus clarki, Rehder and Abbott. This whitish shell is 1 to 1½ in. (25 to 38 mm) high, similar to *C. austini,* but Clark's cone has strongly beaded cords at the shoulders. It is rare and is found in moderately deep water in the Gulf of Mexico. $350

Carrot Cone
Conus daucus, Hwass. The color of this solid shell varies from dark orange to bright yellow with some specimens having a light yellowish central band. It is 1 to 2 in. (25 to 51 mm) high, and the spire is usually marked with white blotches on the orange background. This uncommon shell is found in moderately deep water from Florida to the West Indies. .... $5–$75

Florida Cone
Conus floridanus, Gabb. The color of this shell is variable, usually white with broad patches of orange or yellow and a white band on the body whorl. It is 1½ to 1¾ in. (38 to 44 mm) high with an elevated spire, a sharp apex, and a distinct suture. This common shell is found on sand from the low-tide line to moderately shallow water from North Carolina to both coasts of Florida. ..... $4–$12

Dark Florida Cone
Conus floridanus floridensis, Sowerby. This cone is 1½ to 1¾ in. (38 to 44 mm) high, similar to *C. floridanus* but darker and with dominant rows of brown dots. Moderately common, it is found on sand from the low-tide line to moderately shallow water from North Carolina to both coasts of Florida. .... $3–$16

Burry's Cone
Conus floridanus burryae, Clench. The body whorl of this subspecies is brown and the spire is light with brown lines on the whorls. It is 1½ to 1¾ in. (38 to 44 mm) high and is uncommon, found in fairly shallow water in the Florida Keys. $20

Glory-of-the-Atlantic Cone
Conus granulatus, Linné. The shoulders of this shell are rounded so that the spire lacks the pointiness of most cones. It is 1 to 1¾ in. (25 to 44 mm) high. The surface is marked with distinct spiral lines, and the color is variable from orange to pink with spiral brown markings and a band around the middle of the body whorl. The shell is rare, found on reefs in moderately deep water from the Florida Keys to the West Indies. .... $48–$650

Jasper Cone

Conus jaspideus, Gmelin. This gray shell has evenly spaced spiral cords with rows of brown and white dots and a rather high-pointed spire. It is ½ to ¾ in. (13 to 19 mm) high, very common, and found in sand in shallow water from North Carolina to Florida and the West Indies and to Brazil. . . . . $1–$18

Julia's Cone

Conus juliae, Clench. This shell is pinkish with a rather broad white band around the body whorl. It is 1½ to 2 in. (38 to 51 mm) high and has rounded shoulders, a short spire, and an overall pattern of fine lines and dots. This rare shell is found in moderately deep water from Florida to the West Indies. . . . . $12–$60

Mouse Cone

Conus mus, Hwass. The shell is gray with reddish brown spots, and it usually has a light band around the middle of the body whorl. The surface sculpture is faint spiral cords, and the height is 1½ to 2 in. (38 to 50 mm). The shell is common on sand or reefs in the intertidal zone from southeast Florida to the West Indies. . . less than $1–$4

Conus peali, Green. This ½ to ¾ in. (13 to 19 mm) high shell is similar in appearance to *C. jaspideus,* except the color pattern is more subtle. Many malacologists regard this shell as merely a color variant of *C. jaspideus.* The shell is uncommon and is found in sand in shallow water from southern Florida to the West Indies. $4

Pearled Cone

Conus pennaceus, Born. The color of this shell is variable, but it is generally orange brown with white spots and triangular patches. The shell is solid and is 2½ in. (64 mm) high. It has a moderately raised spire. It is fairly common on reefs in Hawaii. . . . . $3–$85

Puzzling Cone

Conus perplexus, Sowerby. The gray or pinkish surface of this species is covered with tiny brown dots and has three reddish brown bands. It is 1 in. (25 mm) high, and the pointed spire is heavily marked with brown and white blotches. The shell is common in moderately shallow water from the Gulf of California to South America. . . . . less than $1–$10

Prince Cone
Conus princeps, Linné. The yellow-brown shell is marked with irregular brown lines running up and down the body whorl. It is 2 ½ in. (64 mm) high and has a low spire and a thick brown periostracum. Fairly common, it is found in moderately shallow water from the Gulf of California to Ecuador. . . . . $5–$45

Conus pygmaeus, Reeve. This white shell, usually with dark reddish markings, has a high spire and is 1 to 1½ in. (25 to 38 mm) high. Fairly common, it is found from Florida to the West Indies. The albino specimen is uncommon. . . . . $2–$4
Albino $9

Conus ranunculus, Hwass. This large colorful cone is 2 to 3 in. (51 to 76 mm) high and is white with reddish brown markings. It is common in Florida and the West Indies. . . . . less than $1–$2

Crown Cone
Conus regius, Gmelin. The light-colored cone is marked with reddish brown or purplish mottled patches, sometimes creating a banded appearance. It is 2 to 3 in. (51 to 76 mm) high and has knobs on the spire. This shell is common, found on reefs from southern Florida to the West Indies and Brazil. . . . . $6–$30

Regular Cone
Conus regularis, Sowerby. This pale white shell with orange-brown spots has a pointed spire and is 2 to 2 ½ in. (51 to 64 mm) high. Fairly common, it is found in shallow water from the Gulf of California to Panama. $2–$5

Sennott's Cone
Conus sennottorum, Rehder and Abbott. This smooth white shell has spiral rows of reddish brown dots and a prominent spire with a sharp apex. It is 1 to 1½ in. (25 to 38 mm) high. This uncommon shell is found in deep water in the Gulf of Mexico. . . . . $60–$200

Sozon's Cone

Conus sozoni, Bartsch. The light orange shell has two prominent white bands, which have spiral lines made up of brownish dots on the body whorl, and the rest of the shell is marked with reddish brown splotches. It is 2 to 4 in. (51 to 102 mm) high and has a well-developed spire with a sharp apex. This uncommon shell is found in deep water from South Carolina to Florida and the Gulf of Mexico. . . . . $5–$18

Alphabet Cone

Conus spurius atlanticus, Clench. This cone is the Florida subspecies of the alphabet cone. It is 2 to 3 in. (51 to 76 mm) high, has a flat top with a short spire, and is creamy white with spiral rows of orange and brown spots and blotches. The species has a thin light-brown periostracum. It feeds on worms and is fairly common in sand in shallow water from Florida to the West Indies. $5–$60

The Caribbean form, *Conus spurius spurius*, Gmelin, has darker blotches arranged in more obvious bands. $4–$27
More than 3 in. (80 mm) $75

A color variant, *Conus spurius aureofasciatus*, Rehder and Abbott, occurs, marked with bands of yellow or orange brown. . . . . $35–$45

Stimpson's Cone

Conus stimpsoni, Dall. This yellow or white shell usually has 2 or 3 yellowish bands around the body whorl. It is 1½ to 2 in. (38 to 51 mm) high and has a well-formed spire. It is uncommon, found in deep water from southeast Florida to the Gulf of Mexico. $40

Warty Cone

Conus verrucosus, Hwass. This pinkish gray shell has reddish brown blotches and regularly placed beads on the revolving ribs. It is ¾ to 1 in. (19 to 25 mm) high. The shell is common in shallow water from southern Florida to the West Indies and Brazil. . . . . $1–$5

Repreentatives of this family have a long slender many-whorled shell with a clawlike operculum that distinguishes them from the similarly shaped members of the *Turritellidae* family, which have a round operculum. These carnivores live in sandy mud or coral sand in shallow water, where they feed on sea worms.

Gray Atlantic Auger
Terebra cinerea, Born. This gray or brown shiny shell has numerous small ribs extending vertically halfway down from the sutures on each volution. It is 1 to 2 in. (25 to 51 mm) high and has a small aperture. The shell is common in sandy shallow water from southern Florida to the West Indies and Brazil. . . . . $1–$3

Common Auger
Terebra dislocata, Say. The color of this shell varies from pale gray to orange brown with darker bands of gray and brown. It is 1 to 2 in. (25 to 51 mm) high. The shell has a spiral band just below each suture and numerous axial ribs on each suture. It is common in sand in shallow water from Virginia to Florida and the Gulf of Mexico and to the West Indies. . . . . less than $1–$20

Florida Auger
Terebra floridana, Dall. This rather large shell, 3 in. (76 mm) high, is yellowish white, and the whorls have a raised line around the middle and two rows of axial ribs around the top. The shell is rare, found in shallow water from South Carolina to Florida. . . . . $10–$20

Shiny Atlantic Auger
Terebra hastata, Gmelin. Also listed as *Hastula hastata.* This species is not as sharply tapered as other augers. It is 1 to 1½ in. (25 to 38 mm) high and glossy tan with a creamy band below the suture. The shell is uncommon, found in shallow water from southern Florida to the West Indies. . . . . $1–$2

Terebra strigata, Sowerby. The height of this auger is 4 in. (102 mm); the shell is tan with prominent vertical brown streaks. There is a slight indentation below the well-defined sutures. This shell is uncommon, found on sand in moderately shallow water from the Gulf of California to Panama. . . . . $3–$15

Flame Auger

Terebra taurinum, Lightfoot. Formerly classified as *T. flammaea,* Lamarck. This shell is our largest auger; it reaches a height of 6 in. (152 mm) or more. It is yellowish white with rows of reddish brown streaks. This uncommon shell is becoming rarer due to overcollecting. It is found in moderately shallow water from southern Florida and the Gulf of Mexico to the West Indies. ... $5–$20

Turrets { Family :: Turridae }

Also known as turrids and slit shells, members of this family are spindle shaped, and the outer lip usually has a slit or notch. Generally deep water snails, there are hundreds of species; little is known about them, so there is much dispute regarding their classification.

Elegant Star Turret

Ancistrosyrinx elegans, Dall. Up to 2 in. (51 mm) high, this yellowish white shell has a long open canal and sharply angled volutions with prominent shoulders. There are short spines on the shoulders, and the surface has rows of very tiny beads. This rare shell is found in deep water in southern Florida and the West Indies. $60

Sanibel Turret

Crassispira sanibelensis, Bartsch and Rehder. The shell is less than 1 in. (25 mm) high. It is pale brown to reddish brown and has a ridge at the suture. It is common, found in moderately shallow water in southern Florida and the Gulf of Mexico. .... less than $1–$13

Giant White Turret

Polystira albida, Perry. This white shell has a long open canal, a light brown periostracum, and a brown clawlike operculum. The shell is 3 to 4 in. (76 to 102 mm) high and has a distinct notch on the outer lip. At one time, it was considered rare; it is now frequently found by shrimp fishermen in deep water in southern Florida and the Gulf of Mexico. .... $2–$5

Delicate Giant Turret

Polystira tellea, Dall. This shell is similar to the giant white turret, but its sculpture is not as defined. It is grayish or white and is 2 to 3 in. (51 to 76 mm) high. It has a light brown periostracum. The shell is fairly common in deep water in southeast Florida. .... $1–$8

Obelisk Shells { Family :: Eulimidae }

These shells have a high spire, which is generally slightly bent to one side. The surfaces are polished, and the animals are parasites.

Obelisk Shell
Niso hendersoni, Bartsch. This polished tan or yellowish shell is 1 in. (25 mm) high. Its suture is marked with darker brown. It is uncommon and is found in the southeastern part of the United States. .... $15–$65

Pyramid Shells { Family :: Pyramidellidae }

These pyramid- or cone-shaped shells are usually highly polished. Many of the representatives of this family are tiny. They are found on sandy bottoms, and many are parasites.

Giant Atlantic Pyram
Pyramidella dolabrata, Lamarck. This shell is a large representative of this genus. It is 1 in. (25 mm) high and is cream white with spiral brown lines on the whorls. The sutures are deeply impressed on this solid shell. The species is common, found on sand in shallow water from Florida to the West Indies. .... $2–$3

Lined Bubble Shells { Family :: Hydatinidae }

These snails have thin, rounded, and inflated shells with an involute spire. The animal is large, usually extending outside the shell.

Brown-Lined Paper Bubble Shell
Hydatina vesicaria, Lightfoot. The shell is large, 1 to 1½ in. (25 to 38 mm), and is white to tan with many thin wavy brown lines around the shell. The large colorful animal is rust colored with a blue border. The shell is fairly common in sand in shallow water from southern Florida to the West Indies. .... $5–$20

True Bubble Shells { Family :: Bullidae }

These oval-shaped shells are thin and lightweight. They are rolled like a scroll with a wide open aperture. They are carnivores, found in sand and mud bottoms.

Bubble Shell
Bulla amygdala, Bruguière. This brownish shell has rows of darker brown spots and is ¾ to 1 in. (19 to 25 mm) high. It is common off the west coast of Florida and the West Indies. $1

California Bubble Shell

Bulla gouldiana, Pilsbry. The large shell is 1½ to 2½ in. (38 to 64 mm) high. This oval grayish brown shell has dark streaks edged with white. It has a thin brown wrinkled periostracum. It is common, found on mud flats at night from the low-tide line to moderately deep water in southern California and the Gulf of Calilfornia. . $1–$3

Paper Bubble Shells { Family :: Atyidae }

These small thin shells favor muddy brackish waters. The animal is large and extends beyond its shell.

Paper Bubble Shell or Elegant Glassy Bubble

Haminoea elegans, Gray. This almost transparent shell is thin and fragile. It is ⅓ to ¾ in. (9 to 19 mm) high, yellowish or cream in color, and very glossy. It is common in shallow water from southeast Florida to the West Indies. . . . . $1–$5

Sowerby's Paper Bubble

Haminoea virescens, Sowerby. This small transparent shell is about ½ in. (13 mm) high. It is greenish yellow and has a thin outer lip. This shell is uncommon, found among rocks in shallow water from the Puget Sound to Mexico. . . . . less than $1–$2

Marsh Snails { Family :: Ellobiidae }

The shape of these shells varies from conical to round. The shells lack an operculum. The snails spend a considerable amount of time out of water, since their gills have been replaced by a modified lung; however, even though they breathe air, they stay near salt water.

Coffee Bean Snail

Melampus coffeus, Linné. This brownish gray shell has 3 white bands on the body whorl. The shell is top shaped and has a gray periostracum. It is ½ to ¾ in. (13 to 19 mm) high and has a thin strong shell and low spire. These snails serve as food for wild ducks. They are common in intertidal areas in mud near mangroves from southern Florida to the West Indies. . . . . less than $1–$2

Amphineura

Chitons { Families :: Chitonidae, Lepidochitonidae }

The shell of the chiton is made up of 8 overlapping individual plates (valves), which form a shield. The plates are connected by a leathery "girdle" that extends around the plates to form a border. The muscular foot comprises the entire underneath side of the animal. Chitons are nocturnal and are found in rocky areas near shore. They feed on decaying vegetation and some animal matter.

Common West Indian Chiton

Chiton tuberculatus, Linné. The color varies from brown to gray, and occasionally the shell can be marked with green, black, or white. It is 2 to 3½ in. (51 to 89 mm) long, and the prominent girdle is scaled similar to snakeskin. This shell is common in the intertidal zone from Florida to Texas and to the West Indies. ...... $2–$5

Lined Red Chiton

Tonicella lineata, Wood. The shiny plates are yellowish brown with all or some of the plates decorated on the sides with reddish brown lines. The shell is 1 in. (25 mm) long and is found under stones near shore from Alaska to San Diego, California; the shell is common on the shores of Alaska but uncommon in California. ...... $3–$12

Scaphopoda

Tusk Shells { Family :: Dentaliidae }

The animals in this class are covered by a slightly curved tubular shell, which is open at both ends. They are found in sand with the smaller end sticking upward, while the tough burrowing foot extends from the broad end. The tapered shape of the shell suggests the common name, tusk shell. They are usually white but can be pale pink or green and are found in sandy bottoms from the intertidal zone to great depths.

Ivory Tusk Shell
Dentalium eboreum, Conrad. This thin shell is gently curved and is 2 in. (51 mm) long. It is white, occasionally with a pinkish or yellowish cast. The shell is common in shallow water from North Carolina to Florida and to the West Indies. .... less than $1–$2

Class: Cephalopoda

Paper Nautiluses & Spirula
{ Families :: Argonautidae, Spirulidae }

The class *Cephalopoda* includes the most highly evolved mollusks, including the shell-less octopuses and squids, and the nautiluses and spirulas. The nautilus is very similar to the octopus. It has 8 tentacles, and in the case of the female, two of these arms are modified to produce egg cases and the shell. The female can reach a length of 24 in. (610 mm) and produces a shell about 14 in. (350 mm) long, but the male is shell-less and only about ½ in. (13 mm) long. However, the female is not permanently attached and can discard the shell at any time.

Paper Nautilus

Argonauta argo, Linné. The thin shell is white with brown markings around the edge of the early part of the shell. The flat shell reaches a diameter of 8 in. (203 mm). This worldwide pelagic animal is found mostly as empty shells washed on shore from New Jersey to Texas, but primarily off Florida. . . . . $10–$225

Brown Paper Nautilus

Argonauta hians, Lightfoot. The fragile shell is tan or light brown and is 2 to 3 in. (51 to 76 mm) in diameter. Found worldwide in warm seas, it is occasionally thrown on beaches by storms, primarily off the coasts of Florida and southern California. . . . . $1–$12

Spirula

Spirula spirula, Linné. The animal is a squidlike creature with 8 arms and 2 tentacles. It is 1½ in. (38 mm) long. This animal produces a white spiral shell, ½ to 1 in. (13 to 25 mm) across, which it uses as protection, withdrawing its arms and tentacles into the shell when frightened. The live animal lives at depths of 600 to 3,000 ft. (183 to 915 m), and the shell floats to the surface when the animal dies and the flesh decays. . . . . less than $1–$2

Class:
Pelecypoda

Nut Shells { Family :: Nuculidae }

Shells in this family are thin and have a pearly inside and distinct sharp inter-locking teeth along the hinge. They are usually three-cornered or oval in shape.

Atlantic Nut Shell

Nucula proxima, Say. This whitish shell has a thin olive-green periostracum, is almost triangular in shape, and is $1/4$ to $3/8$ in. (6 to 10 mm) long. The interior is pearly, with triangular hinge teeth. The shell is common in mud from Maine to Florida and Texas. $1

Nut Shells { Family :: Nuculanidae }

These shells are usually elongated with a rounded front, and they are extend-ed on the other end. They have 2 lines of hinge teeth separated by a large chondrophore.

Pointed Nut Clam

Nuculana acuta, Conrad. This small shell is $1/2$ in. (13 mm) long and is white with a thin brownish or greenish periostracum. The shell has concentric grooves and is pointed on the posterior end. It is common from Massachusetts to Florida and the West Indies.   . $1–$3

Ark Shells { Family :: Arcidae }

Shells in this family are usually heavily ribbed, have a heavy dark periostracum, and lack bright coloration. These strong shells have a hinge that is straight with many small teeth arranged in a line on both valves. Some have a large ventral gape in the shell to accommodate the huge byssus. They can be found attached to undersides of rocks or, in the case of those that lack the byssus, buried in sandy mud.

Incongruous Ark

Anadara brasiliana, Lamarck. This shell is $1^1/2$ to 2 in. (38 to 51 mm) long and about as high. The left valve is larg-er and overlaps the other. The shell is white and has strong ribs marked with crossing lines. The periostracum is thin and brown. The shell is common, found from North Carolina to Florida, Texas, and the West Indies. . . . . less than $1–$2

Cut-Ribbed Ark
Anadara lienosa floridana, Conrad. Formerly classifed as *A. secticostata,* Reeve. This sturdy white shell is 3 to 5 in. (76 to 127 mm) long with radiating ribs. The periostracum is brown. The shell is common and is found from North Carolina to Florida, Texas, and the West Indies. $2

Eared Ark
Anadara notabilis, Röding. The sturdy shell reaches a length of 3½ in. (89 mm), the beaks are well elevated, the anterior end is short and rounded, and the longer posterior end is squarish. The shell is white with radiating ribs crossed by fine lines. The periostracum is brown. Young shells have an obvious dorsal ear. The species is common from South Carolina to Florida and the West Indies and to Brazil. .... $1–$10

Blood Ark
Anadara ovalis, Bruguière. This clam is one of the very few mollusks that has red blood, thus its common name. The shell is 2 in. (51 mm) long and is white with the bottom half covered with a greenish brown thick periostracum. Its surface has radiating ribs, and the prominent beaks almost touch at the tips. The shell is common from Massachusetts to Florida and Texas and to the West Indies. .... $1–$3

Mossy Ark
Arca imbricata, Bruguière. Previously classified as *Arca umbonata,* Lamarck. The surface of this 1½ to 2 in. (38 to 51 mm) long shell is irregularly crisscrossed by growth lines. It is purplish white inside and out but is covered with a dark brown mossy periostracum. It is common from North Carolina to Florida and to the West Indies. .... $1–$2

Turkey Wing
Arca zebra, Swainson. This yellowish white shell is marked with irregular reddish brown zebralike stripes. The shell is 2 to 4 in. (51 to 102 mm) long and has a moderately large gape, an olive-green byssus, and a thick shaggy periostracum, which obscures the stripes on live specimens. It is common from North Carolina to Florida, the West Indies, and Brazil. .... $1–$2

Red-Brown Ark

Barbatia cancellaria, Lamarck. This shell is reddish brown with the surface marked with many fine radiating lines; the interior is brown. The shell is 1 to 2 in. (25 to 51 mm) long and has a hairy periostracum. It is common from Florida to the West Indies. . . . . $1–$2

White-Bearded Ark

Barbatia candida, Helbling. The surface of this shell has numerous ribs crossed by growth lines. The shell is 1 to 2 in. (25 to 51 mm) long and is yellowish white with a shaggy yellowish brown periostracum. It is common from North Carolina to Florida, Texas, and the West Indies. . . . . $1–$2

Doc Bale's Ark or Stout Ark

Barbatia tenera, C. B. Adams. About 1½ in. (38 mm) long, this thin white shell has a thin brown periostracum and a sculpture of fine radiating lines. It is found in moderately shallow water from southern Florida to the West Indies. . . . . $1–$3

Ponderous Ark

Noetia ponderosa, Say. A thick shell with strong ribs, it is 2½ in. (64 mm) long. The shell is white and has prominent beaks that point backwards. In life, it has a heavy, almost black periostracum. It is common from Virginia to Florida and Texas. . . . . less than $1–$2

Bittersweet Clams { Family :: Glycymeridae }

Members of this family are solid, round, and well-inflated shells. The hinges have curved rows of teeth. They are colorful. Living shells have a thin velvet like periostracum that covers most of the shell except near the center of the valves. The distance between the beaks and the direction they turn aid in identification of these clams.

Giant American Bittersweet

Glycymeris americana, DeFrance. This shell is dull gray or tan and grows up to 5 in. (127 mm) long. It is circular and rather compressed, with beaks pointing toward each other. This uncommon shell is found in moderately shallow to deep water from North Carolina to Florida and Texas. . . . . $2–$4

Bittersweet Clams (continued)

Decussate Bittersweet
Glycymeris decussata, Linné. The cream-colored shell is blotched with brown, has numerous radiating lines, and is 1 to 2 in. (25 to 51 mm) long. The beaks point toward the rear of the shell. Fairly common, it is found in moderately shallow water from southeast Florida to the West Indies. .... $1–$3

Glycymeris gigantea, Reeve. Another large bittersweet, this clam reaches a length of 4 in. (102 mm). It is round and cream colored with reddish brown mottlings, usually in a zigzag pattern. The shell is uncommon, found in shallow water from the Gulf of California to Acapulco, Mexico. .... $3–$10

Comb Bittersweet
Glycymeris pectinata, Gmelin. This small shell, ½ to 1 in. (12 to 25 mm) long, is white or gray with bands of brown spots. It has well-rounded radiating ribs. The shell is common, found on sand and gravel in shallow water from North Carolina to Florida and Texas and to the West Indies. .... $1–$2

Mussels { Family :: Mytilidae }

Members of this family are the true mussels. They are characterized by thin strong pear-shaped shells, a long hinge line, sharp beaks, and shiny interiors. They can be found attached to rocks by the byssus or attached to underwater objects in communities, forming barriers. Mussels are found in all seas but do best in cool waters. Most are edible.

Scorched Mussel
Brachidontes exustus, Linné. The elongated gray shell has a yellowish brown periostracum and is 1 in. (25 mm) long. The surface is ribbed, more prominently near the margins. The shell is common, often found washed ashore attached to shells and seaweed. It is found in moderately shallow water from Cape Hatteras to Florida and to the West Indies. $1

Hooked Mussel
Brachidontes recurvus, Rafinesque. The valves of this bluish black shell are triangular and curved. The surface has fine elevated lines that divide as they near the posterior end. This 1 to 2 in. (25 to 51 mm) long shell is common, found in shallow water from Cape Cod to Florida and to the West Indies. $1

Giant Date Mussel

Lithophaga antillarum, d'Orbigny. This elongated cylindrical shell is 2 to 4 in. (51 to 102 mm) long and has low beaks and no hinge teeth. It is brown and has a thin brown periostracum. Immature species are found hanging from rocks by the byssus; adults bore into limestone and other soft rocks. Fairly common, the shell is found in shallow water from southern Florida to the West Indies. . . . . less than $1

Scissor Date Mussel

Lithophaga aristata, Dillwyn. This light brown mussel is easily identified by the pointed tips of the valves that cross each other at the posterior end. The elongated shell of this rock borer is 1 in. (25 mm) long. Fairly common, the shell is found in soft rocks in moderately shallow water from southern Florida to the West Indies and Brazil and from southern California to Peru. . . . $3–$4

Tulip Mussel

Modiolus americanus, Leach. Previously classified as *Modiolus tulipa,* Lamarck. The thin strong shell is usually a light brown, but some specimens have fine rose or purple rays; the periostracum is brown. The anterior end is narrow, while the posterior end is wide. The length is 2 to 4 in. (51 to 102 mm). The shell is very common in communities found attached to broken shells and rocks in moderately shallow water from North Carolina to Florida and to the West Indies. $1

California Mussel

Mytilus californianus, Conrad. This dark brown or bluish black shell is large, attaining a length up to 10 in. (254 mm). It has many irregular radiating ribs and is triangular in shape with the beaks forming a pointy apex. The shell is very common, found on rocks in the intertidal area from the Aleutian Islands to California and to Mexico. . . . . $1–$2
190 mm+ . . . . $12–$15

Common Blue Mussel

Mytilus edulis, Linné. The bluish black shell has a shiny clear periostracum. It reaches a length of 3 in. (76 mm) and is triangular shaped with a surface marked by growth lines. This mussel is used as food. Very abundant, it is found in crowded colonies attached to rocks and wharves by strong byssal threads. The shell has an extensive range; it is found in the intertidal zone from Greenland to South Carolina, California, and Europe. . . . . less than $1–$3

Members of this family are inequivalve and have an opening under the right valve for the byssus. The tropical species include the valuable pearl oysters that produce gem quality pearls. All species produce mother-of-pearl. Layers of this nacre cover a grain of sand or other small irritant in the mantle, producing a pearl. The larger more valuable pearls are produced by oysters in Caribbean waters. The pearl oysters are found on rocks, sea fans, and other fixed objects.

Atlantic Wing Oyster

Pteria colymbus, Röding. The shell is purplish brown with brown radiating lines and has a pearly interior. It is fairly solid, has a straight hinge line, and is 1½ to 3 in. (38 to 76 mm) long. The matted spiny periostracum is usually rubbed off of more mature specimens. The left valve is inflated, and the right is flattened. The shell is common, found in shallow water attached to sea fans and sea whips from North Carolina to the West Indies and Brazil. . . . . $1–$2

underside

Western Wing Oyster

Pteria sterna, Gould. Similar to the Atlantic wing oyster, this shell is purplish brown with lighter brown rays and has a long posterior wing, differentiating it from the Atlantic species. The western wing oyster was once a commercial source for mother-of-pearl. The shell is 3 to 4 in. (76 to 102 mm) long and has a wrinkled periostracum. Fairly common, it is found among weeds in muddy shallow water from California to Panama. $1–$6

Atlantic Pearl Oyster

Pinctada radiata, Leach. The color of this shell varies, but it is usually some shade of brown or green. The shell is flat, thin, and brittle. It is 2 to 3 in. (51 to 76 mm) long and has a tan periostracum, occasionally with long fine spines if the specimen is found in quiet waters. The shell is common in shallow water attached to rocks and sea fans from southern Florida to the West Indies and Brazil. . . . . $1–$3

Flat Oysters & Tree Oysters { Family :: Isognomonidae }

Characterized by vertical parallel grooves on the external hinge area, these oysters are compressed or flattened with one valve flatter than the other. They are thin shelled and smooth, although in some cases, they have concentric plate-like growth lines. They can be almost circular or oval, or they can be elongated into a hammerlike shape. The flat oysters attach themselves to undersides of rocks, crevices, and mangrove roots by means of a byssus.

Flat Tree Oyster

Isognomon alatus, Gmelin. Valves of this almost circular shell are extremely flat and are marked with growth lines that may be smooth or rough. The color varies from brown, black, or purplish, and the shell is 2 to 3 in. (51 to 76 mm) long. It is common, found in large clumps on mangrove roots, pilings, or submerged brush in shallow water from southern Florida to the West Indies and Brazil. $1

Lister's Tree Oyster

Isognomon radiatus, Anton. Previously classified as *I. listeri.* This elongated shell, irregular in shape, reaches a length of 3 in. (76 mm). It has flat wrinkled valves and is greenish brown. The shell is common under rocks and in crevices from the low-tide line to moderately shallow water from southeast Florida to the West Indies and to Brazil. . . . . less than $1

Pen Shells { Family :: Pinnidae }

These shells are large and wedge shaped with thin shells that gape at the posterior end. They are found partially buried in sand, attached by a strong byssus. Some species attain a length of more than 2½ ft. (762 mm).

Stiff Pen Shell

Atrina rigida, Lightfoot. This large delicate shell can attain a length of 12 in. (305 mm). The triangular shell is dark brown, and the valves have many rows of tubelike spines on slightly elevated ribs. The shell has a strong silky byssus. Fairly common, it is found in shallow muddy water from North Carolina to Florida and the West Indies. $2

Scallops { Family :: Pectinidae }

All scallops were previously classified in one genus, *Pecten*. However, because of the great diversity of the members, many genera have been derived for classification of this family. Scallops usually are inequivalve, having a strongly convex lower valve and a flat or concave upper valve. The surface usually bears ribs, and the margins of the valves are scalloped. In live specimens, the outer edge of the mantle has a row of tiny eyes, each with a cornea, lens, and optic nerve. Juveniles are sedentary, usually fixed by a byssus. Most adult species however, are capable of swimming by rapidly opening and closing the valves. This movement propels the scallop through the water—backwards—with the hinge end trailing. The large mussel that controls this movement of the valves is the part people eat when they have "scallops." Several species are commercially valuable as food.

Calico Scallop

Aequipecten gibbus, Linné. These little scallops are extremely variable in color—the upper valve can be a mixture of white, rose, purple, brown, and yellow orange; the bottom valve is usually whitish with flecks of color. The shell's length is 1 to 2 in. (25 to 51 mm), the wings are equal, and the valves have many radiating ribs crossed by growth lines. This scallop is harvested commercially for food. It is common in shallow water from North Carolina to Florida and the Gulf of Mexico and to the West Indies. . . . . . $1–$7

Tryon's Scallop

Aequipecten glyptus, Verrill. This pinkish brown shell has a darker color on the radial flutings. Its length is 1 to 2½ in. (38 to 51 mm). The valves are concave. The right valve and the interior are white. This uncommon shell is found from south of Cape Cod to Florida and the Gulf of Mexico. . . . . $2–$12

Atlantic Bay Scallop

Aequipecten irradians, Lamarck. Pictured is *A. i. irradians*, an east coast subspecies. The length of the shell is 2 to 3 in. (51 to 76 mm), the wings are equal, and the valves are convex. The grayish brown subspecies has rounded radiating ribs and mottlings on both similarly colored valves. This species is the common commercial scallop of the east coast. This common shell is found in eelgrass from Nova Scotia to Florida. . . . . less than $1–$3

The Gulf subspecies *A. i. amplicatus*, Dall, is found in the Gulf of Mexico. It is mottled gray to black with a white lower valve. The shell is very inflated. It is common in Texas. . . . . $1–$2

Another subspecies, *A. i. concentricus*, Say, is not pictured. It is more brightly colored, usually with an orange-brown to bluish gray upper valve and a light-colored lower valve. The shell is common from New Jersey to Florida and along the Gulf coast to Louisiana. . . . . less than $1–$3

Wavy-Lined Scallop

Aequipecten lineolaris, Lamarck. The shell is tan with wavy concentric lines and prominent dark spots and is 1 to 2 in. (25 to 51 mm) long. It is uncommon; its range is from the Florida Keys to the West Indies. . . . . . $2–$6

Rough Scallop

Aequipecten muscosus, Wood. The many ribs on the valves are very heavily scaled, the shell is sturdy, the wings are unequal, and the length is 1 to 2 in. (25 to 51 mm). The color is variable from tan to orange to reddish brown and, rarely, bright lemon yellow. The shell is moderately common in fairly shallow water from North Carolina to Florida and the West Indies. . . . . $1–$4
Orange $15
Yellow $8

Spathate Scallop

Aequipecten phrygium, Dall. This flat, fan-shaped shell is 1 in. (25 mm) long. The valves are gray with irregular pinkish bands and have prominent ribs. The shell is rare, found in deep water from Cape Cod to eastern Florida and to the West Indies. . . . . $30–$75

Pacific Pink Scallop

Chlamys hastata hericius, Gould. The shell is almost round with the front wings twice as large as the hind wings and is 2 to 3¼ in. (51 to 83 mm) high. The valves can be white, yellow, orange, or purple, usually with paler colors on the rays or marked by purple rings. The shell is fairly common on rocks, in sand or mud, or in sponges from the low-tide line to deep water from southern Alaska to California. . . . . $1–$6
Orange $35

Little Knobby Scallop

Chlamys imbricatus, Gmelin. The length is 1 to 1¾ in. (25 to 44 mm). The valves of this shell are usually flat and white, sometimes with patches of pink, and the margins and hinge area are purplish. The wings are unequal, and the ribs have regularly spaced hollow knobs. This rare shell is found in moderately shallow water from southern Florida to the West Indies. . . . . $6–$15

Mildred's Scallop

Chlamys mildredae, Bayer. This tan to brown shell with strong radiating ribs and unequal wings is about 1 in. (25 mm) long. It is rare, found from southeast Florida to the Gulf of Mexico and off Bermuda. . . . . $25–$125

Ornate Scallop

Chlamys ornatus, Lamarck. This small shell, 1 to 1¼ in. (25 to 32 mm) long, has wings that are extremely unequal—one is barely discernible. Strongly ribbed, the shell is brown, tan, or white with brown or red spots. This uncommon shell is found in shallow water from southern Florida to the West Indies. . . . . $3–$12

Sentis Scallop

Chlamys sentis, Reeve. The valves of this species are quite flat with many fine ribs, and the front wings are 4 to 5 times larger than the hind wings. The shell is 1 to 1½ in. (25 to 38 mm) long, and the color varies from orange to purplish or yellowish. The shell is common, found attached to undersides of rocks from North Carolina to the Florida Keys and the West Indies. . . . . $1–$3

Benedict's Scallop

Chlamys benedicti, (unpictured) Verrill and Busch. It is similar to the sentis scallop but is smaller and has larger hind wings. It is found from southern Florida to Texas and is not as common as the sentis scallop. . . . . $2–$10

Giant Rock Scallop

Hinnites multirugosus, Gale. Also classified as *Hinnites giganteus,* Gray. The shell is reddish brown to light gray with the colors fading as the shell grows. This scallop begins life as a free-swimming bivalve but becomes sessile, attaching itself by the lower valve to rocks. The shell is thick with many small scaly ribs, oysterlike in appearance, and 3 to 10 in. (76 to 254 mm) long. It is common, found on rocks from the low-tide line to moderately shallow water from the Aleutian Islands to Baja California. . . . $3–$45

Antillean Scallop

Lyropecten antillarum, Récluz. This small shell is usually less than 1 in. (25 mm) long and has thin, rather flat valves with quite widely spaced ribs. Its color may be light yellow, pale orange, or tan, occasionally with white mottlings. Fairly common, it is found in shallow water from southern Florida to the West Indies. Colored shells are rare. . . . . $2–$13

Colors $20

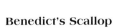

Lion's Paw

Lyropecten nodosus, Linné. This heavy shell is reddish brown to orange. It is 4 to 6 in. (102 to 152 mm) long and has strong ribs with prominent raised knobs. The shell is a prized collector's item. While it is fairly common, only single shells are usually found washed up on shore. The shell is found in moderately deep water from North Carolina to Florida and the Gulf of Mexico and to the West Indies and Brazil. . . . . $4–$175

Giant Pacific Scallop or Weathervane Scallop

Pecten caurinus, Gould. The valves are flat, thick, and solid and have broad sturdy ribs. The wings are equal. The shell reaches a length of 6 to 8 in. (152 to 203 mm). The upper valve is purplish red, and the lower valve is pink or white. This species is fished commercially. Fairly common, it is found in moderately deep water from Alaska to Humboldt Bay, California. . . . . $8–$10

Pecten laurenti, Gmelin. The upper valve is slightly convex and is tan or light reddish brown with white mottlings; the lower valve is more convex and white. The wings are about equal, and the shell is 2½ in. (64 mm) long. This uncommon shell is found in the Gulf of Mexico and the Caribbean. . . . . $2–$8

Paper Scallop

Pecten papyraceus, Gabb. The upper valve is flat, glossy, smooth, and reddish brown; the lower valve is white with a rim of yellow on the inside and occasionally on the outside of the valve. The shell is 2 in. (51 mm) long and does not have ribs. Fairly common, it is found in moderately deep water from the Gulf of Mexico to the West Indies. . . . . $4–$8

Ravenel's Scallop

Pecten raveneli, Dall. The shell is pink to purple and only occasionally orange. The upper valve is flat with dark irregular markings; the lower valve is convex and has many widely separated grooved ribs. It is 2 in. (51 mm) long and has unequal wings. This uncommon shell is found in moderately shallow water from North Carolina to the West Indies. . . . . $1–$4
Purple/orange . . . . $5–$12
Albino $10

Tereinus Scallop

Pecten tereinus, Dall. This small scallop, about 1 in. (25 mm) long, is grayish white or buff with irregular tan markings. It is uncommon, found from southern Florida to the Gulf of Mexico. $5–$17

Scallops (continued)

Zigzag Scallop
Pecten ziczac, Linné. The length of this shell is 2 to 4 in. (51 to 102 mm). The upper valve is flat, has many compressed ribs, and is blotched and marked with zigzag black lines; the lower convex valve has low ribs and is mottled reddish brown. The shell is common in moderately shallow water from North Carolina to Florida and the West Indies and to Bermuda. . . . . $1–$25

Atlantic Deep-Sea Scallop
Placopecten magellanicus, Gmelin. This shell is large, 5 to 8 in. (127 to 203 mm) long. The valves are flat and roughened with many narrow radiating ribs. The wings are equal. The upper valve is reddish or pinkish brown; the lower valve is a warm white. This common species is fished commercially. It is found in moderately deep water from Labrador to North Carolina. . . . . . $4–$18
Albino . . . . $15–$40

File Shells { Family :: Limidae }

These oval shells have long colorful sticky tentacles protruding from the shell in the live specimens. Usually they have only one wing and gape open on one side. They can swim in the manner of the scallops, but forward, hinge first. However, they are usually sedentary.

Spiny File Shell or Spiny Lima
Lima lima, Linné. This white shell with many spined ribs is 1 to ½ in. (25 to 38 mm) long. The byssal gape is small, and the anterior wing is larger. The shell is common from southeast Florida to the West Indies. . . . . $1–$3
120 mm+ . . . . $12–$40

Delicate File Shell
Lima scabra tenera, Sowerby. This thick oval shell is 1 to 3 in. (25 to 76 mm) long, and the surface has numerous small ribs, giving the shell a satinlike luster. It is white, with a thin yellow-tan periostracum. The shell is common from Florida to the West Indies. . . . . $1–$3

The rough lima, *Lima scabra scabra*, (unpictured) Born, has many ribs, which are covered with small spines. $2–$8

Spiny Oysters { Family :: Spondylidae }

Most members of this family live attached by their right valves to rocks in shallow to moderately deep water. Like the scallops, they have eyes along the edge of the mantle. The shells develop long spines, usually in quiet waters.

Atlantic Spiny Oyster or **Thorny Oyster**
Spondylus americanus, Hermann. The color is variable from white to brown and occasionally yellow or red. The heavy shell is 3 to 5 in. (76 to 127 mm) and is covered with radiating ribs and spines. Although these shells are common, the specimens found on beaches or in coral are usually badly worn. The shells are found on coral from Florida to the West Indies. .... $9–$50

Spondylus gussoni, Da Costa. This brown spiny shell is 2 to 4 in. (51 to 102 mm) long. It is found in the Gulf of Mexico. .... $7–$13

Cat's Paws { Family :: Plicatulidae }

These small thick shells are identified by the broad radiating ribs or folds. They are found on rocks and coral, where they are attached by either valve.

Cat's Paw or **Kitten's Paw**
Plicatula gibbosa, Lamarck. Usually 1 in. (25 mm) long or smaller, this white shell has pencil-like gray or reddish lines on the radiating folds. Most are white because the sun bleaches them. The shells are very common from North Carolina to Florida and to the West Indies. .... $1–$2

Oysters { Family :: Ostreidae }

These shells are extremely irregular in shape and have unequal valves. They are usually fixed by the lower valve to some solid object. They produce nonvaluable pearls.

Ostrea cristata, Born. This Carribean species of oyster is 1 to 2 in. (25 to 51 mm) long. .... $1–$15

Crested Oyster
Ostrea equestris, Say. The oval-shaped shell is 2 in. (51 mm) long, whitish, and covered with a brown or grayish purple periostracum. It is common from Virginia to Florida and Texas and to the West Indies. $1

Oysters (continued)

on
stem
with
barnacle

Coon Oyster
Ostrea frons, Linné. The shape of this oyster is variable: it is long when attached to stems and rounded when on rocks. The shell is reddish to deep brown and 1½ to 2 in. (38 to 51 mm) long. It is common from North Carolina to Florida and to the West Indies. .... $1–$10

Native Pacific Oyster
Ostrea lurida, Carpenter. The shape of the shell varies, but it is usually small, 2 in. (51 mm) long, with a rough surface and crude growth lines. The brownish gray oyster is excellent eating. It is common from Alaska to Baja California. $1

Sponge Oyster
Ostrea permollis, Sowerby. This oyster lives in the sponge, *Stellata sp.* It is 1 to 3 in. (25 to 76 mm) long and is whitish or tan with irregular wavy ridges and a thick soft periostracum. The shell is common from North Carolina to Florida and the West Indies. .... $2–$3

Giant Pacific Oyster
Crassostrea gigas, Thurnberg. This large gray or tan shell can be up to 12 in. (305 mm) long. It is variable in shape, usually elongated with coarse surface sculpture. Native to Japan, it was introduced in Hawaii and can be found from British Columbia to California. .... $1–$4

Eastern Oyster
Crassostrea virginica, Gmelin. This species is the most important commercial oyster. It is 3 to 6 in. (76 to 152 mm) long and is dark gray. The shell is rough and heavy. Its shape varies depending on its position as it grows, often in dense colonies. The shell is common from New Brunswick to Florida and the Gulf of Mexico; it was introduced on the Pacific coast of the U.S. ..... $1–$3

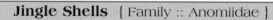

Jingle Shells { Family :: Anomiidae }

These thin translucent clams have a stalklike byssus that fixes the shell through a hole in the lower valve. When the animal dies, the cuplike upper valve is washed ashore.

Jingle Shell
Anomia simplex, d'Orbigny. The color varies from dull yellow to coppery red or even gray or black. The shell is 1 to 2 in. (25 to 51 mm) long. It is common from Nova Scotia to Florida and to the West Indies. ...... $1–$3

Arctic Clams { Family :: Arcticidae }

This family has many fossil genera but only one surviving species. The shells are large, thick, and circular and have a thick periostracum. They live buried in sand with only the end of the short siphon exposed.

Black Clam or Ocean Quahog

Arctica islandica, Linné. The large whitish shell is up to 4 in. (102 mm) long has a dark wrinkled periostracum. It is common; large colonies are dredged in moderately deep water from the Arctic Ocean to North Carolina. $7–$8

Marsh Clams { Family :: Corbiculiidae }

These clams favor brackish water and are eaten by waterfowl. The thick inflated shells can be round or triangular.

Carolina Marsh Clam

Polymesoda caroliniana, Bosc. This shell is olive to greenish brown and has a thin brown periostracum. It is round and 1 to 2 in. (25 to 51 mm) long. This common shell is found in mud from Virginia to Florida and to Texas.
. . . . less than $1

Astartes { Family :: Astartidae }

These bivalves have an external ligament and distinct lunule. They are sculptured with concentric grooves. Most have a tough brown periostracum.

Boreal Astarte

Astarte borealis, Schumacher. This white shell is solid, oval, and 1 to 2½ in. (25 to 64 mm) long. The periostracum is usually frayed at the margins. The shell is common from the Arctic Ocean to Massachusetts and to Alaska. $1

Crassatellas { Family :: Crassatellidae }

These clams are solid with equal valves and strong hinges.

Gibb's Clam

Eucrassatella speciosa, Adams. This brown shell has a thin brown periostracum. It has many dense packed ridges. The shell is 2 in. (51 mm) long with a round anterior and a ridge on the hind end. It is common from North Carolina to Florida and to the West Indies. . . . . $1–$2

Carditas { Family :: Carditidae }

These usually solid, equivalve, and strongly ribbed shells have a strong triangular tooth under the right umbo.

Broad-Ribbed Cardita
Cardita floridana, Conrad. The white or grayish shell has raised beaded radial ribs with reddish brown spots; the periostracum is gray. The shell is 1 to 1½ in. (25 to 38 mm) in size. It is common from Florida to Texas and to Mexico. $1

Lucines & Buttercups { Family :: Lucinidae }

These shell are usually round and rather thick. They are white or yellowish. They live in sand or mud where the animal constructs a mucus-lined tube to draw water and food and expels wastes through a siphon.

Buttercup Lucine
Anodontia alba, Link. This white shell has fine concentric growth lines and orange bands. The interior has an orange cast. The shell is 1½ to 2 in. (38 to 51 mm) long and is common from North Carolina to Florida, the Gulf states, and the West Indies. $3

Chalky Buttercup
Anodontia philippiana, Reeve. Previously listed as *A. schrammi* or *Loripinus schrammi*, Crosse. The shell is white with fine concentric lines. It is 2 to 4 in. (51 to 102 mm) long. The interior is colorless. This species is common from North Carolina to the West Indies. .... less than $1

Californian Lucine
Codakia californica, Conrad. Also listed as *Epilucina californica*. The shell is dull white with many fine concentric ridges. It is 1 to 2½ in. (25 to 64 mm) long. This shell is common from southern California to Baja California. .... $7—$8

Tiger Lucine
Codakia orbicularis, Linné. This white shell is marked with many fine radiating ribs crossed by raised growth lines. It is 2½ to 3½ in. (64 to 89 mm) long and may have a pink border on the inside. The shell is common from Florida to the West Indies. $2

Cross-Hatched Lucine

Divaricella quadrisulcata, d'Orbigny. This white shell is 1 in. (25 mm) long and has parallel grooves running diagonally across the surface. It is common in moderately shallow water from Massachusetts to Florida and to the West Indies. $1

Northeast Lucine

Lucina filosus, Stimpson. Previously listed as *Phacoides filosus.* The white shell is 1 to 3 in. (25 to 76 mm) long and has compressed valves with widely spaced concentric ridges. This species prefers cold water. It is common from Newfoundland to Florida. . . . . less than $1

Florida Lucine

Lucina floridana, Conrad. The shell is white with a thin yellow periostracum and is 1½ in. (38 mm) long. The thick valves have fine concentric lines. It is common in shallow water in the Gulf of Mexico. . . . . . less than $1

Thick Lucine

Lucina pectinatus, Gmelin. Previously listed as *Phacoides pectinatus.* This heavy yellowish white shell is 1½ to 2 in. (38 to 51 mm) long and has fine concentric ridges and an obvious fold on the hind end. It is common from North Carolina to Florida and to the West Indies. less than $1

Pennsylvania Lucine

Lucina pensylvanica, Linné. The shell is white with a pale yellow or tan periostracum. It has widely spaced concentric ridges and a deep fold from the beak to the posterior margin. The shell is 1 to 2 in. (25 to 51 mm) in size. It is common from North Carolina to Florida and to the West Indies. . . . . $1–$2

Jewel Boxes { Family :: Chamidae }

Jewel boxes are thick heavy shells that have unequal valves and sometimes produce long spinelike projections similar to the spiny oysters. They live attached to rocks, corals, shells, or other solid objects by means of the larger and more convex fixed valve.

Leafy Jewel Box

Chama macerophylla, Gmelin. The color of this shell varies from yellow and pink to rose. It is 1 to 3 in. (25 to 76 mm) long, and the surface has large, scalelike projections with tiny radial lines. It is common, found in shallow to moderately shallow water from North Carolina to the West Indies. . . . . $1–$15

Jewel Boxes (continued)

Clear Jewel Box
Chama pellucida, Broderip. Also classified as *Chama arcana*. Usually white or cream, this shell can be tinged with pink or orange, with the overall appearance of the shell being translucent. It is 1½ to 3½ in. (38 to 89 mm) long and has numerous leafy concentric ridges with irregular leafy projections. This common shell is found attached to rocks and pilings in shallow to moderately deep water from Oregon to Peru. . . . . $2–$13

Smooth-Edged Jewel Box
Chama sinuosa, Broderip. This shell is always white, usually with a greenish interior. It is 2 to 2½ in. (51 to 64 mm) long and is very similar to the leafy jewel box except the margin inside of the valves is smooth. This uncommon shell is found on coral reefs in moderately deep water from southern Florida to the West Indies. $2–$4

Caribbean Spiny Jewel Box
Echinochama arcinella, Linné. Also listed as *Arcinella arcinella*. This yellowish white shell is about 1 in. (25 mm) long and usually has a pinkish tinge on the inside of the valves. It is common, found in shallow water from the West Indies to South America. . . . . $2–$12

Florida Spiny Jewel Box
Echinochama cornuta, Conrad. Also listed as *Arcinella cornuta*. About 1½ in. (38 mm) long, this shell is very similar to the Caribbean spiny jewel box, but it is larger. It is white with the interior often having tinges of red. This shell is common in shallow water from North Carolina to Florida and Texas. $2

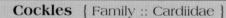

Cockles { Family :: Cardiidae }

When viewed from the end, these bivalves are heart shaped. The valves are equal with serrated or scalloped margins and often gape at one end. They are edible and are popular as food in Europe.

Nuttall's Cockle
Clinocardium nuttalli, Conrad. The shell is whitish or yellowish with a light brown or yellowish brown periostracum. This large, almost circular shell is 2 to 5½ in. (51 to 140 mm) long. The beaks are high, and the valves are sculptured with strong ribs. The shell is common, found in moderately shallow water from the Bering Sea to San Diego, California. . . . . $4–$10

Giant Atlantic Cockle

Dinocardium robustum, Lightfoot. This rather heavy, inflated shell is 3 to 5 in. (76 to 127 mm) long. The valves have regularly spaced strong ribs and rounded beaks. The color is yellowish or tan with irregular spots; the interior is rose. This shell is common, found in moderately shallow water or washed up on shore from Virginia to Florida and Texas. $3

Common Heart Cockle

Dinocardium robustum vanhyningi, Clench and Smith. This subspecies of the giant Atlantic cockle is generally larger, more colorful, and more triangular in shape than *D. robustum*. It is very common, found in moderately shallow water off the west coast of Florida. . . . . $1–$3

Giant Pacific Egg Cockle

Laevicardium elatum, Sowerby. One of the largest cockles, this shell reaches a length of 6 in. (152 mm). The thin valves are inflated and have weak radiating ribs, giving the yellow shell a rather smooth surface. Fairly common, it is found in moderately shallow water from southern California to Panama. . . . . $4–$15

Egg Cockle

Laevicardium laevigatum, Linné. The thin shell is inflated, 1 to 2 in. (25 to 51 mm) long, and white with concentric bands of yellow orange. The surface is smooth with slight traces of ribs. The periostracum is thin and brownish. Occasional colorful specimens may be found, but most are white. The shell is common, found in moderately shallow water from North Carolina to both coasts of Florida and to the West Indies. . . . . less than $1–$5

Morton's Egg Cockle

Laevicardium mortoni, Conrad. This shell is small, ³/₄ in. (19 mm) long, and yellowish white with occasional streaks of orange. The thin shell is inflated and has a slightly pebbled surface. It is common, found in sandy mud from the low-tide line to moderately shallow water from Cape Cod to both Florida coasts and to the West Indies. $1

Ravenel's Egg Cockle

Laevicardium pictum, Ravenel. Some specimens of this white smooth shell are marked with brown zigzag streaks. The well-inflated shell is small, ³/₄ in. (19 mm) long. Fairly common, it is found in moderately shallow water from South Carolina to Florida and the West Indies. . $1–$2

Cockles (continued)

Little Egg Cockle
Laevicardium substriatum, Conrad. This shell is another small cockle, about 1 in. (25 mm) long. The valves are thin, inflated, and quite smooth. The color is yellowish brown with a yellow interior spotted with purple. The shell is common, found in moderately shallow water from Catalina Island, California, to Baja California. $1

Spiny Paper Cockle
Papyridea soleniformis, Bruguière. The interior and exterior of this shell are white or pink, mottled with rosy brown; rare specimens are orange. The shell is 1½ in. (38 mm) long and is thin and flat with numerous fine radiating ribs. Fairly common, it is found in shallow water from North Carolina to Florida and to the West Indies. $1–$5

Prickly Cockle
Trachycardium egmontianum, Shuttleworth. The surface has deep radiating ribs that end in sharp scales. The shell is thin, oval, well inflated, 2 to 2½ in. (51 to 64 mm) long, and yellowish. There are rare albino specimens. The shell is common, found in sand in shallow water from North Carolina to Florida. . . . . $1–$5

West Indies Prickly Cockle
Trachycardium isocardia, Linné. The shell reaches a length of 3 in. (76 mm) and is yellow with irregular brown blotches. It has strong radiating ribs with sharp scales. This common shell is found in shallow water in the West Indies. $1

Magnum Cockle
Trachycardium magnum, Linné. This white or cream-colored shell is marked with yellowish brown patches and is sculptured with deep radiating ribs. It is 2 to 3½ in. (51 to 89 mm) long. This uncommon shell is found from the lower Florida Keys to the West Indies. . . . . $2–$6

Yellow Cockle or Lemon Cockle
Trachycardium muricatum, Linné. The shell is almost round and is yellowish white, occasionally with light speckles. It is strongly inflated and is 2 in. (51 mm) long. It has spiny radiating ribs. The periostracum is brown. This very common shell is found in shallow water from North Carolina to Florida and Texas and to the West Indies. . . . . $1–$5

Atlantic Strawberry Cockle

Trigoniocardia media, Linné. Also listed as *Americardia media*. The surface of this cream-colored shell is checkered with brown to reddish brown and has strong rounded radiating ribs. The length is 1 to 2 in. (25 to 51 mm). The shell is common, found in shallow to moderately deep water from North Carolina to Florida and to the West Indies. .... $2–$5

The western strawberry cockle, *Trigoniocardia biangulata* or *Americardia biangulata*, Broderip and Sowerby (not pictured), is similar to the Atlantic strawberry cockle but is found off California. .... less than $1–$3

Hard-Shelled Clams { Family :: Veneridae }

The hundreds of species in this very large family have certain obvious characteristics: the shells are porcelain-like, equivalve, and egg- or heart-shaped; the beaks point toward the anterior; the ligament is external; the hinge is strong; and each valve has three cardinal teeth. Many have beautiful sculpture and are brightly colored. They burrow and are usually found just below the surface of the sand. These clams are an important commercial food fishery.

Pointed Venus

Anomalocardia cuneimeris, Conrad. This thin wedge-shaped shell is ¾ in. (19 mm) long. The color varies from grayish to greenish or brownish. It has many concentric ribs and is pointed at one end. The shell is common from southern Florida to Texas. .... less than $1

Rigid Venus

Antigona rigida, Dillwyn. Also *Ventricolaria rigida*. This yellowish gray shell is mottled with brown and is 1½ to 2½ in. (38 to 63 mm) long. It has alternating concentric ribs and smaller lines. The shell is common from southern Florida to the West Indies. $1

Queen Venus

Antigona rugatina, Heilprin. Also *Ventricolaria rugatina*. This shell is yellowish white with brown mottlings and is 1 to 1½ in. (25 to 38 mm) long. It has concentric ribs separated by two fine lines. The shell is rare and is found from North Carolina to Florida and the West Indies. .... $5–$8

Empress Venus

Antigona strigillina, Dall. This cream-colored shell is 1½ in. (38 mm) long. It has raised concentric ribs crossed by many fine radiating ribs. The shell is uncommon, found from South Carolina to Florida and the West Indies. $4

Hard-shelled Clams (continued)

Glory-of-the-Sea Venus
Callista eucymata, Dall. The shell may be shiny white to shiny pale brown with reddish brown marks. It is 1 to 1½ in. (25 to 38 mm) long and has flat concentric ribs. This rare shell is found from North Carolina to Florida, Texas, and the West Indies. .... $2–$5

Common California Venus
Chione californiensis, Broderip. The shell is gray with concentric ridges and radial ribs. It is 1½ to 3 in. (38 to 76 mm). This shell is common from California to Panama. .... $2–$3

Cross-Barred Venus
Chione cancellata, Linné. This whitish gray shell is 1 to 1½ in. (25 to 38 mm) and has concentric and radial ribs. It is common from North Carolina to Florida and to the West Indies. .... $1–$2

Beaded Venus
Chione granulata, Gmelin. The shell is gray with dark mottlings and has close scaly radiating ribs. It is 1 in. (25 mm) long. The species is common from southern Florida to the West Indies. .... $1–$2

Lady-in-Waiting Venus
Chione intapurpurea, Conrad. This whitish thick shell has concentric ribs that are wrinkled on the hind end. It is 1 to 1½ in. (25 to 38 mm). The shell is common from North Carolina to Florida, the Gulf states, and the West Indies. .... $1–$2

Imperial Venus
Chione latilirata, Conrad. This polished grayish white shell with brown and purple marks has large broadly rounded concentric ribs and is 1 to 2 in. (25 to 51 mm) long. It is common from North Carolina to Florida, Texas, and the West Indies. .... $1–$3
Albino .... $3–$4

Chione mazycki, Dall. The grayish white shell is 1 to 1½ in. (25 to 38 mm) and has brown spots and concentric ribs. It is found from North Carolina to Florida. $2–$3

King Venus
Chione paphia, Linné. This shiny gray shell is marked with purple and brown and is 1½ in. (38 mm) long. The shell has narrower concentric ribs than the imperial venus. Fairly common, it is found from southeast Florida to the West Indies. .... $2–$6

Elegant Dosinia

Dosinia elegans, Conrad. The white shell has many concentric ridges and is 2 to 3 in. (51 to 76 mm). It is common in the Gulf states. . . . . $1 or less

Calico Clam

Macrocallista maculata, Linné. This shell is tan, checkered with brown, and 2 to 3 in. (51 to 76 mm) long. Fairly common, it is found from North Carolina to Florida and the West Indies. . . . . $1–$4

Sunray Venus

Macrocallista nimbosa, Lightfoot. The pinkish gray shell with darker radiating markings reaches 6 in. (152 mm). It is common from North Carolina to Florida and Texas.
. . . . $2–$5

Quahog or Cherrystone Clam

Mercenaria mercenaria, Linné. This valuable commerical clam attains 5 to 6 in. (127 to 152 mm). The thick shell is dull gray, often with a purple border. It is very common from the Gulf of St. Lawrence to Florida; it was introduced in California. . . . . $1–$2

Two subspecies include *Mercenaria mercenaria notata,* Say, which is brightly colored with zigzag marks, and the fatter Texas quahog, *Mercenaria mercenaria texana,* Dall. $1–$4

Princess Venus

Periglypta listeri, Gray. Previously listed as *Antigona listeri.* This thick grayish white shell is 2 to 4 in. (51 to 102 mm) and has radial ribs and concentric ridges. It is found from Florida to the West Indies. . . . . $2–$3

Royal Comb Venus

Pitar dione, Linné. The pale violet or white shell has a long ridge at the posterior. It is 172 in. (38 mm) long. This species is common from Texas and Florida to the West Indies. . . . . $4–$8

Pitar lupanaria, Lesson. This shell is similar to *P. dione,* but it is 2 in. (51 mm) and it has concentric ribs. It is uncommon, found from the Gulf of California to Peru.
. . . . $3–$8

Pacific Littleneck

Protothaca staminea, Conrad. This cream to brown shell may have brownish mottlings. It is 2 in. (51 mm) and has many concentric and radial ribs. The shell is common from Alaska to Baja California. . . . . $1–$2

Hard-shelled Clams (continued)

Washington Clam
Saxidomus nuttalli, Conrad. The shell is grayish white with irregular brown lines and is up to 5 in. (127 mm). It has fine sharp concentric ribs. The shell is common in California. $1

Trigonal Tivela
Tivela mactroides, Born. This triangular yellowish brown shell with darker radiating rays is 1 in. (25 mm) long. It is common in the West Indies. . . . . $1–$3

Rock Dwellers { Family :: Petricolidae }

The mollusks in this family burrow in clay, shale, coral, or limestone, creating a cavity that is enlarged as the clam grows to full adult size. Large communities of these shells can cause erosion of shore lines. The shells are elongated, have a weak hinge, and gape behind.

False Angel Wing
Petricola pholadiformis, Lamarck. The thin long shell has many strong radiating ribs. It is 2 in. (51 mm) long and chalky white. The species is common in the intertidal zone from Canada to Florida, the Gulf of Mexico, and the West Indies; it was also introduced in Washington and California. . . . . $2–$5

Atlantic Rupellaria
Rupellaria typica, Jonas. Sometimes classified as *Petricola typica*. This strong shell is about 1½ in. (38 mm) long. It is grayish white and plump and has coarse ribs. The shell is common, found burrowed in coral in shallow water from North Carolina to Florida and to the West Indies. . . . . $2–$3

Surf Clams { Family :: Mactridae }

Members of this family are equivalve. They usually gape slightly at the ends and have a spoon-shaped cavity in the strong hinge. The cavity (chondrophore) holds a cartilaginous ligament (the resilium), which keeps the shells slightly separated.

Smooth Duck Clam
Labiosa lineata, Say. Also classified as *Anatina anatina*, Spengler. The shell is off-white and is 3 in. (76 mm) long. It gapes at the posterior end, which has a distinct rib radiating from the beaks. The periostracum is thin and yellowish. This uncommon shell is found from North Carolina to Florida and Texas. . . . . $1–$2

Channeled Duck Clam

Labiosa plicatella, Lamarck. Also classified as *Anatina canaliculata,* Say, and in genus *Raeta,* Gray. This thin and somewhat fragile shell is white or cream and is 2 to 3 in. (51 to 76 mm) long. It has concentric ribs. The shell is common, found in sand in moderately shallow water from North Carolina to Florida, Texas, and the West Indies. .... $1 or less

Common Rangia

Rangia cuneata, Sowerby. Rather triangular in shape, this shell is thick and grayish white with a grayish brown periostracum. It is 1 to 2 in. (25 to 51 mm) long. This common shell is found in brackish water from Maryland to Florida and Texas. $1

Atlantic Surf Clam

Spisula solidissima, Dillwyn. Also classified as *Spisula raveneli,* Conrad. This large yellowish brown shell reaches a length of 7 in. (178 mm) and has a thin olive-tan periostracum. The shell is common, found in sand in moderately shallow water from Nova Scotia to Florida. It is the largest northeast coast bivalve, and it is eaten. $1–$2

A smaller southern subspecies exists: *Spisula solidissima similis,* Say. .... $1–$2

Pacific Gaper Clam

Tresus nuttalli, Conrad. Another large clam, the shell reaches 7½ in. (190 mm) in length. It has a large gap through which it extends its siphons. It is yellowish white with a brown periostracum. The shell is common, found in mud in moderately shallow water from the Puget Sound to Baja California. .... $12–$13

Tellins { Family :: Tellinidae }

Most of the shells in this family are colorful, highly polished, and rounded to elongate in shape. They are sand burrowers and are distinguished by a long slender siphon, which is used to extract detritus from the water; another short siphon eliminates waste.

Faust Tellin

Arcopagia fausta, Pulteney. Also listed as *Tellina fausta.* The white shell is rather heavy, has coarse growth lines, and reaches a length of 4 in. (102 mm). It is a favorite food of octopuses. The shell is common, found in moderately shallow water from North Carolina to Florida and to the West Indies. .... $1–$2

Baltic Macoma

Macoma balthica, Linné. This thin shell is ¾ to 1½ (19 to 38 mm) long. The exterior is dull white and has a thin pale gray-brown periostracum. The shell is common in muddy bays and coves in shallow water from the Arctic Ocean to Georgia and from the Baltic Sea to California. . . . . less than $1–$3

Constricted Macoma

Macoma constricta, Bruguière. This white shell has a thin light yellow-tan periostracum and is 2 in. (51 mm) long. It is common in shallow water from Florida to Texas and the West Indies. . . . . $1–$2

White Sand Macoma

Macoma secta, Conrad. This thin glossy cream-colored shell is oval shaped and reaches a length of 4 in. (102 mm). It is common, found in sand from the intertidal zone to moderately shallow water from Vancouver Island to Baja California. . . . . $1–$3

Crenulate Tellin

Phylloda squamifera, Deshayes. This white or yellowish shell has a sculpture of fine sharp concentric ridges and thornlike crenulations on the posterior dorsal margin. It is 1 in. (25 mm) long and is fairly common in sand in moderately shallow water from North Carolina to Florida. . . . . $2–$3

Atlantic Grooved Macoma

Psammotreta intastriata, Say. Previously classified as *Apolymetis intastriata*. The shell is thin but strong, has a twisted appearance, and is white, occasionally with a yellow cast. It is 3 in. (76 mm) long, moderately common, and found in shallow water from Florida to the West Indies. . . . . $1–$5

Rosy Strigilla

Strigilla carnaria, Linné. The exterior of the shell is a pale rose color that deepens at the beaks; the interior is rosy pink. The shell is less than 1 in. (25 mm) long, rather solid, and circular in outline. This species is common, found in shallow water from North Carolina to Florida and to the West Indies. $1

White-Crested Tellin

Tellidora cristata, Récluz. Easily identified by the large sawteeth along the dorsal margin, this tellin is rather triangular in shape, white, and 1 in. (25 mm) long. It is uncommon, found in mud or sand in shallow water from North Carolina to Florida and to Texas. . . . . $1–$3

Alternate Tellin

Tellina alternata, Say. This oblong shell is 2 to 3 in. (51 to 76 mm) long. The surface has many parallel fine concentric growth lines. The color is usually white or cream, but the shell may be pink or yellow. It is common, found in shallow water from North Carolina to Florida and to southern Texas. $1

Crystal Tellin

Tellina cristallina, Spengler. This thin translucent white shell has concentric lines on the surface, and the posterior ends in a square-shaped upturned tip. It is 1 in. (25 mm) long, uncommon, and found in moderately deep water from South Carolina to Florida, to the West Indies, and to the Gulf of California. . . . . $2–$3

Smooth Tellin

Tellina laevigata, Linné. The surface of the shell is smooth, often glossy, and white with pale orange rays. The shell is 2 to 3 in. (51 to 76 mm) long, and the posterior end is bluntly pointed. This species is uncommon, found in shallow water from Florida to the West Indies. . . . . $5–$7

Rose Petal Tellin

Tellina lineata, Turton. The exterior of this shell is white, often tinged with yellow or rosy pink, with a darker shade at the beaks; the interior may be pink, white, or white tinged with pink or yellow. The shell is ¾ to 1½ in. (16 to 38 mm) long, and the surface has fine concentric lines. The species is common and is used in shellcraft for flower petals. It is found in shallow water from Florida to the West Indies. . . . . $1–$2

Speckled Tellin

Tellina listeri, Röding. Previously classified as *Tellina interrupta*, Wood. The exterior of this shell is white, usually with streaks of purplish brown. It is long and thin and is 1 to 2 in. (25 to 51 mm) long. It has strong, regularly spaced concentric growth lines. The shell is common, found in shallow water from North Carolina to Florida, to the West Indies, and to Brazil. . . . . $1–$4

Tellins (continued)

Great Tellin
Tellina magna, Spengler. This species is our largest tellin, reaching a length of 4½ in. (102 mm). The left valve is white and not as rough as the more colorful right valve, which is yellowish or orange and has fine concentric lines. The shell is uncommon, found in shallow water from North Carolina to Florida and the West Indies. . . . $10

Sunrise Tellin
Tellina radiata, Linné. This creamy white shell has rose-colored bands radiating from the beaks that are also usually visible on the interior. It reaches a length of 3 in. (76 mm), and the surface is very glossy. The shell is common in shallow water from southern Florida to the West Indies.
. . . . less than $1–$5

A plain whitish or yellowish form exists, *T. r. unimaculata*, Lamarck, which lacks the colorful bands. . . . $3–$4

Salmon Tellin
Tellina salmonea, Carpenter. Also classified as *T. nuculoides*. This small shell, ½ in. (13 mm) long, is somewhat triangular. It has a white shiny surface with irregular purplish or reddish brown concentric growth lines. The interior is salmon pink. The shell is common in sand from shallow to moderately deep water from Alaska to California. . . . . $1 or less

Candy-Stick Tellin
Tellina similis, Sowerby. The shell is whitish with short reddish radiating rays and fine concentric growth lines. It is thin, compressed, and 1 in. (25 mm) long. This common shell is found from the intertidal zone to moderately shallow water from southern Florida to the West Indies.
. . . . $1 or less

Bean Clams & Coquinas { Family :: Donacidae }

These clams are generally wedge shaped; they have an elongated and rounded posterior end and a short, sharply sloping anterior end. They live burrowed just below the surface of the sand on slopes of beaches where they move with the tide so that they remain in the ideal wave-washed area.

Caribbean Coquina
Donax denticulata, Linné. This 1 in. (25 mm) long sturdy shell varies in color from brown, violet, or yellow. It may have darker rays and has fine radiating lines on the surface. The shell is common, found in shallow water in the West Indies. $1

Gould's Donax or Bean Clam

Donax gouldii, Dall. This wedge-shaped clam is about 1 in. (25 mm) long. The color varies from white to purple, usually with pink or violet rays. The surface has light radiating lines. The shell is common in the intertidal area from southern California to Mexico. $1

Florida Coquina or Common Coquina

Donax variabilis, Say. The color of this clam is extremely variable: the shell may be white, yellow, pink, purple, or red, and it may have dark rays or concentric colored lines—or both—producing a plaid pattern. The shell is $1/2$ to $3/4$ in. (13 to 19 mm) long. It is very common, found in the intertidal area from Virginia to Florida and Texas. . . . . less than $1

Giant False Coquina

Iphigenia brasiliensis, Lamarck. This buff-colored shell is purplish near the beaks and has a tan periostracum. It is heavy and reaches 3 in. (76 mm) in length. Moderately common, it is found in sand in shallow water from Florida to the West Indies and Brazil. . . . . $2–$4

Sanguin Clams { Family :: Sanguinolariidae }

Members of this family are shallow-water species with long separate siphons, and the shells gape at the siphonal end. Small hinge teeth are present, and the large strong ligament is external. The clams burrow and are found in mud near mangroves or in brackish water.

Gaudy Asaphis

Asaphis deflorata, Linné. This thin strong shell is 2 in. (51 mm) long and has many radiating lines and wavy growth lines. The color is variable: most specimens are purple, but they can be white, yellow, or orange. Fairly common, the shell is found from southern Florida to the West Indies. . . . . $1–$2

Purplish Tagelus

Tagelus divisus, Spengler. The elongated thin shell is fragile and is 1 to $1^{1}/_{2}$ in. (25 to 38 mm) long. The surface is smooth and shiny. The shell is purplish gray with light purple rays; it has a thin yellowish brown periostracum, and the interior is purple. The shell is common from Massachusetts to Florida, Texas, and the West Indies. . . . . $1–$2

Sanguin Clams (continued)

Stout Tagelus
Tagelus plebeius, Lightfoot. This elongated shell is 3 to 4 in. (76 to 102 mm) long. It gapes, and the surface has fine concentric wrinkles. Fresh specimens are white or yellowish with a thin yellowish brown periostracum; dead shells are white. This species is common from Massachusetts to Florida and Texas. .... $1–$4

Semeles { Family :: Semelidae }

The semeles are roundish and only slightly inflated. They have long separate siphons and a large blunt foot without a byssus. They have an external ligament and a chitinous resilium. These bivalves are found in sand or mud, usually in shallow water, although some species are found in deep water. They are good eating but are not harvested commercially.

Southern Cumingia
Cumingia antillarum, d'Orbigny. Also listed as *Cumingia coarctata*. This small white oval shell is only ¾ in. (10 mm) long and has irregular concentric ridges on the surface. Fairly common, it is found in moderately shallow water from southern Florida to the West Indies. $1–$2

Cancellate Semele
Semele bellastriata, Conrad. The surface of this shell has both radiating and concentric lines; the color varies and can be yellowish tan with brownish marks or purplish gray. It is ½ to 1 in. (13 to 25 mm) long, and the shiny interior often is yellow or violet. The shell is fairly common in moderately shallow water from North Carolina to Florida and the West Indies. .... $1–$2

Bark Semele
Semele decisa, Conrad. This heavy large shell is 2 to 4 in. (50 to 102 mm) long and is brownish white tinged with purple. It has coarse concentric wrinkles and a thin brownish periostracum. Dead specimens, lacking the periostracum, will be pinkish brown. The shell is common, found on rocky bottoms in moderately shallow water from southern California to Baja California. . . $4

Purplish Semele
Semele purpurascens, Gmelin. The shell is oval, 2 in. (51 mm) long, and variable in color—pale yellow blotched with purple, brown, or orange. The surface has fine concentric lines. The shell is common, found in shallow water from North Carolina to Florida and to the West Indies. .... $1–$2

Jackknife Clams & Razor Clams { Family :: Solenidae }

The clams in this family are equivalve and generally gape at both ends. The elongated species are the jackknife clams, and the razor clams are the broader species. They are found in sandy bottoms in coastal waters. All are edible.

Small Jackknife Clam

Ensis minor, Dall. This shell reaches a length of no more than 4 in. (102 mm). It is quite fragile. The whitish shell is curved and has a brown or green periostracum. Fairly common, it is found in the intertidal zone from Florida to Texas. .... $1–$3

Many consider this shell to be a subspecies of the larger Atlantic jackknife clam, *Ensis directus,* Conrad.   . $3–$5

Corrugated Razor Clam

Solecurtus cumingianus, Dunker. About 1 to 2 in. (25 to 51 mm) long, this shell gapes and is rectangular. It is whitish in color with a grayish brown periostracum. The shell is uncommon, found in moderately deep water from North Carolina to Florida and Texas. .... $3–$5

Green Jackknife Clam

Solen viridis, Say. This thin elongated shell gapes at both ends, is 2 to 3 in. (51 to 76 mm) long, and has a shiny greenish periostracum. Fairly common, it is found in the intertidal zone from Rhode Island to northern Florida and the northern Gulf of Mexico. .... less than $1–$2

Geoduck Clams { Family :: Hiatellidae }

Valves of these clams are usually unequal and lack color; some are extremely large. These bivalves bore into sponges, coral, and other limestone deposits, but some bury themselves in deep mud.

Atlantic Geoduck

Panopea bitruncata, Conrad. The valve surfaces bear coarse wavy growth lines, and the shell is dull white. It is 4 to 6 in. (102 to 152 mm) long, has large siphons, and is very similar to the larger Pacific geoduck. This uncommon species was at one time believed to be extinct. It is found in moderately shallow water from North Carolina to Florida. .... $6–$10

Geoduck Clams (continued)

Pacific Geoduck
Panopea generosa, Gould. This species is the largest American clam, reaching 8 in. (203 mm) in length. The siphons are large and may stretch to 2 ft. (.6 m) and cannot be completely withdrawn. The surface has concentric wavy growth lines and is dull grayish white. These clams are excellent food; some states have a 3-clam daily limit. This shell is common in mud from Alaska to Baja California. . . . . $15–$18

Soft-Shelled Clams { Family :: Myacidae }

These clams usually have unequal valves that gape. The left valve contains a spoonlike chondrophore.

Soft-Shell Clam or Steamer Clam
Mya arenaria, Linné. This dull tan or grayish shell is 1 to 6 in. (25 to 152 mm) long and lives buried in sand or mud with the tips of the siphons exposed. It is a popular food clam and is fished commercially. The shell is common, found in gravel and mud in the intertidal area from Labrador to North Carolina. . . . . less than $1–$2

Truncate Soft-Shell Clam
Mya truncata, Linné. The posterior end of this shell is truncated and gapes prominently. The shell is 1 to 3 in. (25 to 76 mm) long and is dull white with a tough yellowish tan periostracum. It is common from the Arctic Sea to Massachusetts and to Washington on the west coast. . . . $1–$2

Angel Wings { Family :: Pholadidae }

These clams can bore into wood, coral, and moderately hard rocks, as well as clay and mud. The thin white shells are brittle, gape at both ends, and have a rough abrading sculpture at the anterior end.

Fallen Angel Wing
Barnea truncata, Say. The posterior end of this shell is truncated. The shell is white, 2 to 2½ in. (51 to 64 mm) long, and extremely fragile. It gapes widely. The surface of the valves has longitudinal and transverse wrinkles. The shell is common, found buried in mud in the intertidal zone from Massachusetts to Florida. . . . . . . $1–$2

Angel Wing

Cyrtopleura costata, Linné. Previously classified as *Barnea costata*. This moderately fragile shell is 5 to 7 in. (127 to 178 mm) long and has widely gaping valves, which touch only at the tip near the top. The shell has well-developed radial ribs and concentric ridges. Live specimens have a pale gray periostracum. The shell is usually pure white, but a rare pink-stained form exists. This species is fairly common, but it is subject to overcollecting. Colonies are found in mud in shallow water from Massachusetts to Florida and Texas and to the West Indies. ..... $4–$9

Campeche Angel Wing

Pholas campechiensis, Gmelin. This thin shell is greatly elongated. It is 4 in. (102 mm) long and is white with distinct ribs. The shell is uncommon; single valves are most often found since specimens are rarely collected alive. The shells are found burrowed deep in mud in the intertidal zone from North Carolina to Florida and the Gulf States and to the West Indies and Brazil. .... $10–$30

Glossary

adductor muscle: in bivalves, the one or two large muscles within the shell that open and close the two valves

anterior end: in bivalves, the front end where the foot protrudes from the shell

aperture: in gastropods, the opening in the last whorl that permits the foot and head of the animal to extend from the shell

apex: in gastropods, the tip of the spire; in tusk shells, the small open hind end

beak: in bivalves, the umbo, the earliest formed part of a valve, usually above the hinge

body whorl: in gastropods, the last and largest whorl of the shell

byssus: in bivalves, a bundle of hair-like strands that is used for attaching the shell to rocks, ledges, coral, etc.

calcareous: made of calcium carbonate; shelly, limy

callus: in gastropods, a calcareous deposit, such as enamel covering a portion of the shell

canal: in gastropods, the open channel on the outer lip or at the base of the shell through which the siphon protrudes

cardinal teeth: in bivalves, the largest two or three shell ridges in the hinged portion of the valve, just under the beak

carnivorous: feeding on animal flesh

chink: lengthened groove along the columella

chondrophore: in bivalves, the spoon-shaped shelf in the hinge which contains the cartilaginous resilum

columella: in coiled gastropods, the solid or hollow axis or pillar around which the whorls are formed

cord: a coarse spiral line on the surface of the shell

dextral: turning from left to right; right-handed; aperture on right side of axis

foot: in gastropods, a muscular organ used for locomotion, adhering to a surface, or digging

gape: the space between the valves of a bivalve when they are only partially closed

girdle: in chitons, a band of leather-like muscular tissue that surrounds the valves and holds them together

herbivorous: feeding on plant matter, algae

hermaphrodite: mollusk that functions as and has the organs of both sexes

inequivalve: in bivalves, the sizes of the two shells are not the same

intertidal zone: the area between the high- and low-tide lines; littoral zone

involute: in gastropods, rolled inward from each side

lateral teeth: in bivalves, long, narrow shelly ridges located in the hinge, below the cardinal teeth

left valve: in bivalves, the shell that is on the left when the whole mollusk is viewed on end with the beak facing you and the anterior end up

ligament: in bivalves, an external or internal band of cartilage, usually behind the beaks, that holds the shells together

littoral zone: the area between the high- and low-tide lines; intertidal zone

lower valve: in bivalves, the more deeply cupped of the two shells

lunule: in bivalves, a depressed heart-shaped area located in front of the beaks

mantle: a fleshy organ that encases the vital organs of the mollusk; it usually contains the glands that secrete the shell

margin: the edges of the shell

nacre: the layer of shell that is pearly or iridescent; mother-of-pearl

nuclear whorl: in gastropods, the earliest or first whorl of the shell

operculum: in gastropods, a shelly or horny plate that completely or partially covers the aperture

outer lip: in coiled gastropods, the outer margin of the aperture farthest from the columella

pallial line: in bivalves, the scar on the interior of the shell where the mantle was attached

parietal shield: in gastropods, a shelly thickening or deposit on the parietal wall; perietal callus

parietal wall: in gastropods, the part of the body whorl opposite the outer lip and bordering the upper part of the aperture; the inner lip

penultimate whorl: in gastropods, the next to the last whorl of the shell; the whorl just above the body whorl

periostracum: smooth or fibrous layer that covers all or part of the hard calcareous shell

periphery: in gastropods, the part of the whorl bulging from the axis

plates: in chitons, the eight hard valves which make up the shell; dorsal shield

posterior end: in bivalves, the hind end where the siphons protrude from the shell

proboscis: a tubular extension of the head having a mouth at the end

radula: an organ located in the mouth cavity composed of minute teeth that may or may not be attached by a flexible ribbonlike muscle, which is used for feeding

resilium: in bivalves, a horny padlike cushion located internally in the hinge that causes the shell to spring open when the muscles are relaxed

ribs: lines in the surface of mollusk shells—axial in gastropods and radial in bivalves

right valve: in bivalves, the shell that is on the right when the whole mollusk is viewed on end with the beak facing you and the anterior end up

sculpture: indented or raised markings on the surface of the shell

sessile: permanently attached, unable to move about

shoulder: in gastropods, a flattened part of the whorl below the suture

sinistral: turning from right to left; left-handed; aperture on the left side of axis

siphon: tubelike extension of the mantle that carries water and waste in and out of the mantle cavity

spire: in gastropods, collectively all the whorls above the body whorl

suture: in spiral gastropods, the line or space where one whorl touches another

thread: a fine line in the surface of the shell

umbilicus: in gastropods, a small hollow at the base of the columella which is visible from below

umbo (pl. umbones): in bivalves, the beak or prominent part of the shell above the hinge

upper valve: in bivalves, the flatter of the two shells

valve: in bivalves, one of the two parts of the shell; in chitons, one of the eight plates that make up the dorsal shield

varix (pl. varices): in gastropods, an axial line or ridge that marks the former location of the outer lip, caused by a thickening of the lip during a major growth stoppage

veliger: the most developed larval stage of mollusks that can be egg encased or free swimming

visceral mass: the fleshy body matter of the mollusk which includes the abdominal organs

whorl: in gastropods, a turn or coil in the shell

wing: in bivalves, a flattened projection from one or both sides of the hinge line

Index